COLORING MANDALAS 3

Circles of the Sacred Feminine

S U S A N N E   F.   F I N C H E R

SHAMBHALA
Boston & London
2006

Shambhala Publications, Inc.
Horticultural Hall
300 Massachusetts Avenue
Boston, Massachusetts 02115
www.shambhala.com

9 8 7 6 5 4 3 2 1

First Edition

Printed in Malaysia

⊗ This edition is printed on acid-free paper that meets the
American National Standards Institute Z39.48 Standard.

Distributed in the United States by Random House, Inc.,
and in Canada by Random House of Canada Ltd

Acknowledgments

Many thanks to Peter Turner and Kendra Crossen Burroughs of
Shambhala Publications for their suggestions and support.

Color images used by permission: Judy Chicago, Meinrad
Craighead, Lee Lawson, Shambhala Publications, Collection
of Shelley and Donald Rubin, Collection of Rubin Museum
of Art. The author is grateful to Himalayan Art Resources
(www.himalayanart.org) for assistance.

For information about Susanne Fincher's workshops, retreats,
and other offerings, see the website www.creatingmandalas.com.

Mandalas and the Sacred Feminine

PRAYER TO THE EARTH MOTHER
Oh life-giving, tranquil, fragrant, auspicious Mother—
Breathe upon us,
Place us at the center of the forces that have issued from thy body,
Unite us with the splendid energy of maidens,
With the light that is in males, in heroes,
In horses and the beasts of the forests.
—*Atharva Veda Samhita,* "Hymn to the Earth"
(trans. William Dwight Whitney, quoted in Jayakar, *The Earth Mother*)

This book offers an interactive exploration of the sacred feminine. By realizing our shared inheritance with the makers of these sacred forms, we may also be touched by their deep insights into the ultimate nature of things. Some of the mandalas in this book are adapted from the sacred art of Eastern religions. They are presented here out of their cultural context. Acknowledging that these designs are holy to many, I encourage you to set aside a sacred space and to approach them in an atmosphere of reverence, appreciation, and gratitude.

In a relaxed state of mind you can let the harmonious designs act upon you, just as ancient chants resonate within your body in calming, revitalizing ways. By engaging with the designs through your choice of colors and their applications, you bring the sacred feminine into the present through your own creativity. It can also be rewarding to join with friends in a group to color and talk afterward about what you experienced while coloring.

Coloring mandalas can be a way to invite hidden parts of your self to be known. Through choices of colors, media, and designs that attract you, you can explore your inner self. Noticing which designs you like best—or least—and learning more about the beings associated with them are good ways to go deeper into your personal experience of the sacred feminine. You might enjoy writing an imaginary conversation with a sacred being, or responding to a particularly meaningful design with a poem. You might even be inspired to construct your own mandala of the sacred feminine, following guidelines in the section "For Those Who Wish to Draw a Mandala," following mandala 46 in the coloring section.

Whatever way you choose to color these mandalas, you will find that the kinesthetic activity of coloring geometric patterns is soothing. Coloring mandalas can energize—and also provide a welcome release of energies. Closing your book and putting it away in a special place at the end of a coloring session is a good way to honor the energies stirred by color and movement.

All mandalas celebrate aliveness in a moment of time, even as they point toward the timeless mystery underneath what we know about our self and the universe we inhabit. Coloring a mandala reminds us of our own center and guides us to an experience of the eternal Now, where the polarities and paradoxes of our ordinary human existence are resolved in peaceful wholeness. Like deep wells of refreshing water, mandalas reconnect us with our own inner wellspring, the ground of our being. In this experience of coloring mandalas, may you find yourself attuned to the sacred feminine in ways that are healing, resonant, and enlightening.

Celebrating the Sacred Feminine

In the West it appears that the Goddess has faded into the background, her rituals fragmented and trivialized. The dark half of the Goddess has been renamed the devil and her light half relegated to superstition. With the rise of feminism, however, modern Western women have renewed interest in the "feminine face of God." Some find that envisioning God as a woman helps them to more easily experience a nourishing spiritual connection with the Divine. Some women find spiritual meaning outside traditional religions, in celebrating the cycles of nature as seen in the passing of seasons, the nurturing of growing things, and the "moon time" (menstrual) cycles of women's bodies. For these women, the rich, dark undertones of the sacred feminine serve as a welcome balance to the superficial culture of our day.

A rising tide of devotion to the sacred feminine is seen everywhere in the West today: in women's circles where menopause is celebrated with croning ceremonies; in pilgrimages to ancient Goddess sites in Glastonbury, Crete, and Ephesus; and in the work of women artists whose images reflect their own body sense as beings centered by a generative mystery (see plate 7 in the color section following page 20). And there is heightened interest as well in the "black Madonnas," distinctive paintings and statues of Mary found in Guadalupe, Einsiedeln, and Dijon. The sacred feminine is seen in the growing interest and acceptance of the status of Mary in mainline Christianity; in the appreciation of the biblical Sophia (the Greek name for the feminine personification of Wisdom in the Book of Proverbs and other Jewish wisdom literature); in the movement to reclaim the traditional practices of the old earth-centered religions; and among members of the ecological movement who see it as a sacred obligation to care for the earth as our Mother. At its simplest, contemporary "thealogy"—the study of the Goddess—is the belief that all beings are deeply connected in the web of life.

As the sacred feminine principle, the Goddess is not only manifest outside us. She is an archetypal image of the Great Mother or Mother Nature residing within each one of us, our potential for nurturing, creating, and mothering.

FIGURE 1
The Great Mother Goddess gives birth, supported by her animals. Turkey, c. 6000 B.C.E. (After Gimbutas, p. 107)

Cultivating a relationship with this feminine part of our self helps us to promote balance in the psyche, which in our culture is often overshadowed by the masculine. In this way, we not only experience greater wholeness but also enhance our creativity. In this work, we may find, like many before us, that the circular designs known as mandalas are a helpful support and resource.

C. G. Jung observed that at times of stress accompanying personal growth, adults instinctively return to making circular designs. He called these designs *mandalas,* from the Sanskrit word meaning "sacred circle." Jung understood that creating mandalas offered his patients solace, aiding their psychological reorientation at times of profound, often challenging, change. More than this, he recognized the activity as an integral part of a natural process that he called individuation (the urge to fulfill one's potential for balance and wholeness).

Because the desire for wholeness is shared by all human beings, mandalas appear in many cultures. Eastern mandalas emphasize the idealized, though attainable, experience of enlightenment, yet despite the prescribed structure of Buddhist and Hindu mandalas, they allow for individual artistic elaboration. Western mandalas emphasize the individual's experience and express in graphic form a unique moment in a person's life, yet often incorporate timeless motifs of ancient sacred art. Circles have expressed the sacred feminine from very early times. They are sacred because they elegantly convey the mysteries of life, beginning with the wonder of birth. The rounded forms of the female body were sculpted and carved by prehistoric peoples. Images of women with big hips and breasts full of life-giving nourishment date from 25,000 B.C.E. Birth shrines with circular designs and images of women giving birth date from around 13,000 B.C.E.

A shrine at Catal Huyuk (c. 6000 B.C.E.) in modern-day Turkey is especially rich. Walls, a platform, and low benches in a small room are all stained red. A painting on the east side of the red platform depicts women with legs apart in the birthing position (figure 1). On the west wall, three circles of yellowish white with red centers are outlined in red. It is possible that the circles could represent the cervix, the circular muscle below the uterus that expands to allow the newborn to emerge. Perhaps the shrine served as

FIGURE 2
*Labyrinth pattern used by women in India to focus
concentration during childbirth. (After Khanna, p. 157)*

an actual birthing chamber, a setting designed to provide support for women in labor. Even today, labyrinthine circular designs similar to those at Catal Huyuk are created by women in India to help them concentrate their energies while giving birth (figure 2).

What a miraculous moment it is when a baby emerges from its mother's body; now there are two human beings where only a moment before there was just one. For ancient people, the creative energy of the Goddess came alive in this miracle of birth, when the mother herself personified the Great Mother and Earth Goddess. Modern women, too, respond to this powerful energy, as shown by the return to natural deliveries, midwifery, and breast feeding beginning in the 1960s in the United States. Attending a birth, one witnesses the opening of the vagina transform into a circle as the baby is born. Then perfect nourishment flows in the form of milk from the birth mother's plump breasts. Is it any wonder that the circle became a symbol of the mystery of life, and that women, as those who give birth, made the circle a feminine symbol?

Giving birth is hard work for both mother and baby. In the service of the Goddess, midwifery came into being to assure a good outcome. Still, for women in the past, birth was also a brush with death, and so the duality of the Goddess—life-giving and death-dealing—was present from the beginning of her worship.

For ancient people, it was obvious that the Goddess held their lives in her hands. It was she who generated the rhythms of the seasons, she who held the power of the moon that makes plants grow. She ensured that plenty of healthy young deer, rabbits, and horses were born in the spring. It was she who ruled the ocean, and brought sea creatures into the fishermen's nets, and kept the sea gentle as they harvested their catch. Her springs of clear water offered cool refreshment and miraculous healing, while her rivers and seas were sacred crossing points from this world to the next. It was she who helped a woman hold the affection of a husband or a lover, and she who granted the wish for a child. She it was who presided over life, and the life-giving energies of nature. And it was she who welcomed the dead back into her embrace (see plate 8). The people buried their own in her earthen womb, tucking them in like children after a long, tiring day. The Goddess set all in order—the cosmos and the great round of human existence, birth and life and death. All were her creations.

The notion of the Goddess as the source of nature's cycles is seen in rhythmic patterns that convey energy, movement, and continuity. Some earth-centered religious practices surviving today suggest that the Goddess was found in the steady heartbeat of a drum, the repetitive chanting of sacred syllables, the circling movements of dance, and the rhythmic visual forms of meanders, zigzags, crisscrosses, spirals, and concentric circles. She was part of daily life, as revealed in the motifs of pottery: snakes, flowers, birds, and the Goddess herself, with her wavy hair, her full breasts and owlish eyes, her triangular pubis, and her round, oval, or fish-shaped vulva.

Circles and Sacred Practices

Rolling land, with its flowing water, valleys, and mountains recalls the curves of a woman's body—her hips, breasts, buttocks. Since circular openings are associated with mothers giving birth, it is easy to transpose this significance to caves. Reminiscent of the mother's womb, being inside a cave may have seemed like being in the body of the Goddess, she who births and lovingly cares for all her creatures. In an atmosphere of reverent ceremony, a person stepping forth from a cave is born anew as the child of the Great Mother, perhaps transformed, healed, or initiated into a new understanding of life. Archeological evidence of sacred ceremonies in caves abounds: paintings, pottery, small figures, and carefully-crafted objects.

Originating with simple rituals celebrating the rhythms of nature, increasingly sophisticated observances evolved into worship activities that were codified and transmitted from generation to generation. Patterns of worship were already well established when the creators of the *Rig Veda* (c. 800 C.E.) gathered together, in written form, some of the ancient verses that comprise sacred Hindu texts. Of interest to us, the *Rig Veda* contains the first known use of the word *mandala*. There, a mandala is a collection of verses, something like a chapter in a book, meant to be recited in a particular order. The Sanskrit scholar Jared Klein explains that a mandala is "anything round, a cycle, a wheel, a turning thing." One implication is that the word *mandala* implies harmonious, predictable, repeating cycles and probably traces its origin to earlier ideas of the Goddess as the source of these rhythms.

The notion that circular turning expresses the Goddess's sacred cycles adds yet another dimension to the significance of circles. In the movement of turning, time and energy enliven the static form of the circle. The circle becomes a symbol of the energy source that sets in motion orderly patterns of creation. The circle, then, functions to generate, yet safely contain and regulate, the life force associated with the sacred feminine.

We see these dual functions in the sacred spaces and ritual practices of Old Europe. For example, it is thought that prehistoric circles of standing stones—such as those at Stonehenge, Avebury, and Callanish in the British Isles—are sites where the natural cycles of the Goddess were observed and celebrated. Standing stones are often associated with water and constructed with reference to seasonal alignments of the sun, moon, and stars. The life-death-rebirth cycles of the seasons—and of human life—were venerated in these places, as nearby burial sites attest.

Dance was another a way of creating circles. Evidence is found in ancient pottery in Romania (c. 45,000 B.C.E.) depicting circling dancers touching shoulder to shoulder, hip to hip. It is reported that circle dances performed by women around wells in the old European Goddess tradition were seen in Scotland as late as the nineteenth century. And until the early twentieth century, villagers on the Scottish island of Iona performed a special summer solstice celebration. They ran their horses sunward (clockwise) around a mound that legend said was a fairy castle—perhaps an ancient Pictish (from which the word *pixie* may derive) burial site. The archeologist Marija Gimbutas concludes that "stone rings and ring dances [and other circular movements] seem to be an extension of the centrally concentrated Goddess energy. The circle—be it fairy dance or ring of standing stones—transmits the energy increased by the combination of the powers of stone, water, mound, and circling motion."

Stories of the Sacred Feminine

Few sources have been discovered that survive from a time when the Divine was primarily conceptualized as feminine. Fragments describing some of the pre-Hellenic Greek goddesses survive. The stories are different from the ones usually taught as Greek mythology. It is thought that they predate the arrival of patriarchal influences in Greece. An example is the story of the goddess Gaia, reconstructed by the religion scholar Charlene Spretnak:

> Gaia danced forth and rolled Herself into a spinning ball. She molded mountains along Her spine, valleys in the hollows of Her flesh. From Her warm moisture She bore a flow of gentle rain that fed Her surface and brought life. Wriggling creatures spawned in tidal pools, while tiny green shoots pushed upward through Her pores. She filled oceans and ponds and set rivers flowing through deep furrows. Gaia watched Her plants and animals grow. In time She brought forth from Her womb six women and six men. The mortals thrived but they were continually concerned with the future. When She saw that their worry about the future nearly consumed some of Her children, She installed among them an oracle. Gaia instructed Her priestess in the ways of entering a trance and in the interpretation of messages that arose from the darkness of Her earth-womb. Unceasingly the Earth-Mother manifested gifts on Her surface and accepted the dead into Her body. In return She was revered by all mortals. Many of Her temples were built near deep chasms where yearly the mortals offered sweet cakes into Her womb. From within the darkness of Her secrets, Gaia received their gifts.

The first civilizations of Europe, the Near East, and India are described by Gimbutas as matrifocal, peaceful, earth- and sea-bound cultures. As they were invaded by nomadic northerners with a patriarchal culture and a religion centered on a male sky god, the Goddess was gradually displaced. Gods began to appear alongside goddesses in the stories of the people. In ancient Sumer, the goddess Inanna, First Daughter of the Moon and the Morning and Evening Star, took a husband (figure 3) and relied on her grandfather for some of her powers.

As goddess of the earth and the sky, Inanna regulated the cosmic rhythms and presided over the fertility of the earth and its growing things. She is depicted as strong, independent, intelligent, and passionate in love and war. One story tells of Inanna's descent to the underworld, where she encountered her mysterious dark sister Erishkegal, who cursed her to die. Inanna was released with the intervention of her grandfather Enki, God of Waters and Wisdom.

Sacred marriage rites between Inanna and the god-king Dumuzi were celebrated each new year to assure nature's fertility during the growing season. A sacred text, transcribed by Diane Wolkstein and Samuel Noah Kramer, describes a sensuous interlude Inanna enjoys with her

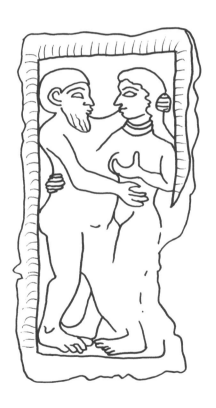

FIGURE 3

The sacred marriage of the goddess Inanna with the god-king Dumuzi was celebrated each new year to assure Nature's abundance. Iraq, 2000–1600 B.C.E. (After Wolkstein and Kramer, p. 43)

bridegroom, Dumuzi. Inanna calls to him, "The bed is ready." The text continues:

He put his hand in her hand.
He put his hand to her heart.
Sweet is the sleep of hand-to-hand.
Sweeter still the sleep of heart-to-heart.

As in the story of Inanna, male images of the Divine became prominent and the devotion once given exclusively to the Great Goddess was bestowed on other deities. Over time, the Great Goddess became numerous goddesses symbolizing the qualities once gathered into one. In her benevolent, nourishing, creative aspect, she is the Great Mother as Danu, Isis, Ceridwen, Inanna, Lakshmi, Parvati, Tara, Kuan Yin, Demeter, and Sophia. As the dark, mysterious, and familiar with death, she is Erishkegal, Kali, Durga, Lilith, Hecate, Medusa, and the Black Madonna. The scholar J. C. Cooper enumerates some symbols of the Goddess: "the crescent moon, crown of stars, blue robe, horns of the cow, the spiral, concentric circles, all waters, fountains, wells, all that is sheltering, protecting, and enclosing—the cave, wall, earth mound, gate, temple, church, house, city—all vessels of nourishment, and breasts as nourishment, all containers of abundance, and all that is hollow and receptive—the cup, cauldron, basket, chalice, horn of plenty, vase, *yoni* (vulva)—all that comes from the waters—shells, fishes, pearls." Among birds, her companions are the dove, swan, goose, crow, and owl. Her creatures include the bear, cow, horse, sow, rabbit, snake, cat, and dog (see mandalas 7–11 in the coloring section). Among her flowers are the lotus, lily, and rose. Trees and their fruits are associated with her, as are groves of trees, stones standing like trees, and pillars suggesting tree trunks. With the rise of Christianity, the old European Goddess religion was discredited, and its practitioners—mostly women—were persecuted, and even killed as witches and heretics. Yet the old Goddess religion, with its lore of healing herbs, midwifery, and earth-centered rituals, persists in surprising ways even into modern times. Carol Christ, a leading feminist theologian, tells the story of discovering a very old myrtle tree, tenderly cared for, in the courtyard of the Orthodox Christian convent of Paliani on the island of Crete. A stone wall enclosed the sacred area

FIGURE 4
Worship of the Goddess in the form of a tree. Egypt,
1550–1295 B.C.E. (After Neumann, 1955, 1963, p. 102)

around the tree, known as the Panagia Myrtia, or "All-Holy Myrtle Tree." The tree was said to perform miraculous cures for petitioners. Testimony to this was given by the many thanks offerings hanging from its branches. A painted image of the Madonna known as the Panagia, "the All-Holy," was nestled in the tree. According to the nuns, the tree was holy because the icon of the Panagia had been found in it. The nuns said the icon had flown there and more than once had been returned to the church, only to be discovered the next morning in the tree. Finally, the nuns understood that the Panagia wanted to be worshiped in the tree (see mandala 14).

Since *Panagia* is in the feminine gender, it may have originally been a name for the Goddess, later applied to the Virgin Mary. Women are shown tending sacred trees in ancient artifacts from long before the compilation of the Genesis story (see figure 4). The Goddess portrayed as a tree is seen on amulets from 3000 B.C.E. found in the Indus Valley. Inanna sings the praise of her holy tree in Sumerian poetry. In Greek tradition, the goddess Aphrodite is associated with the island of Crete, and the myrtle tree is considered hers. It is possible that the Panagia Myrtia might once have been venerated as a prepatriarchal epiphany of the Goddess herself.

In another part of the world we see a similar adaptation of the old ways. Mexico's patroness, the Virgin of Guadalupe, is a popular icon of contemporary Latin American Catholicism. She first appeared in 1523 to Juan Diego, a simple Indian, on Tepeyac Hill near Mexico City. The apparition of a dark Indian maiden wrapped in a blue mantle commanded him to build a church on that spot. When the bishop demanded a sign, Guadalupe directed Juan Diego to gather roses from the garden that had miraculously sprung up at her feet and take them to the bishop. Juan Diego obeyed, and when he opened his serape to let the roses tumble out, the bishop was amazed to see the image of the Virgin on the cloth itself. The Catholic Church accepted the miracle, and a church was built on the spot. But there were those who questioned Guadalupe's sudden popularity only ten years after the Spanish conquest. The historian Frank Waters quotes Father Sahagun writing of his doubts:

> Near the mountains there are three or four places where they used to offer most solemn sacrifices, and to which they came from distant lands. One of these is on a little hill they called Tepeyac, now named Our Lady of Guadalupe. In this place they had a temple dedicated to the mother of the gods whom they called Tonantzin, which means "our mother." Thither they came from far distant regions . . . men, women, boys and girls, and brought many offerings. There were great assemblages and all said, "Let us go to the festival of Tonantzin." Now, the church built there is dedicated to Our Lady of Guadalupe whom they also call Tonantzin, imitating the prelates who called Our Lady the Mother of God (in Aztec), Tonantzin. And so they still come to visit this Tonantzin from afar, as much as before; a devotion which is suspicious because everywhere there are many churches for Our Lady and they do not go to them, but come from great distances here to their Tonantzin as before. [See mandala 13.]

So beneath the dark-faced Madonna the ancient Tonantzin, mother of the Aztec gods, reveals herself. Goddess of the earth and corn, she came again to her people, wrapped in her mantle of sky blue, on the site of her ancient temple. She came in December, just before the rains, when she was honored with festivities long before the Spanish came. So the ancient goddess is present in modern forms even when she is denied—or forbidden—by official doctrine. As Carol Christ conjectures, "When Christianity prohibited Her worship, the Goddess went to the places where She could still be honored and revered. The images and names are different, but the devotions, prayers, and the offerings have changed little in thousands of years."

The Virgin Mary—she of the Immaculate Conception, mother of Jesus, she of the white lilies, of the fragrant roses, of the white dove, and the crescent moon—is an important symbol of the sacred feminine in Christianity. It is she who helps redeem mankind from the eternal suffering brought on by the Fall into sin, mortality, and pain—set loose by Eve's unfortunate decision to eat fruit from the Tree of Knowledge of Good and Evil. Although she is considered mortal in traditional church doctrine, Mary shares many attributes in common with the Goddess as loving mother. Like Kuan Yin, the feminine Bodhisattva of Compassion in Buddhism, Mary is compassionate and hears the prayers of all the people, no matter how poor. She intercedes on their behalf, both with her son Jesus and with God the Father.

Her story shares themes with the stories of many goddesses. For example, the conception of a divine son by a mother without a husband is found in the story of the Egyptian goddess Isis. Her son, the god Horus, was conceived with the dismembered phallus of her dead husband Osiris. The Phrygian goddess Nana, a virgin, impregnated herself by putting an almond or a pomegranate in her bosom. She gave birth to a son, the god Attis. Mary's sacrifice of her beloved son and his triumphant resurrection resonate with earlier stories of the death and renewal of a god-king, such as those of Dionysus, Tammuz, Adonis, Attis, Osiris, and Dumuzi.

An important distinction between the Virgin Mary and the Goddess is the traditional idea that the Virgin stands above or outside the physical plane, often symbolized in ecclesiastical art by her standing upon the crescent moon, an ancient symbol of life's flux and flow. Her officially

FIGURE 5
Rainbow Goddess arcs around the center of Navajo sand painting, an example of a mandala. The black cross in the center is said to be logs whirling in a circular motion. (After Jung, 1959, 1969, p. 96)

endorsed position as a woman who puts right what Eve did wrong has contributed to a Western cultural split between the physical and the spiritual. The devaluing of the physical in preference for the noncorporeal, spiritual—and intellectual—realms, has led to the point of view that matter is dirty, profane stuff useful only as a resource that can be exploited or refined into something better or more useful. Because women are embedded in the physicality of life by the natural rhythms of menstruation, pregnancy, childbearing, and the allure attributed to them, they have been relegated to the dark "Eve" side of the equation, which is seen as less important, wrong, or even bad.

The urge of contemporary believers, set in motion by the feminist questioning of traditional Western culture, is toward a positive valuation of womanhood. In this process, Mary has proven a source of inspiration for many. The feminist philosopher Mary Daly points out that Mary's virginity provides a positive image of independence, challenging the patriarchal view that women are defined only by their relationships to men. Further, the Assumption of Mary into heaven to a place of honor can even be viewed as an acceptance and endorsement of her physicality by God and his son. Above all, Mary is appreciated as a counterbalance to the exclusively masculine God in Christian tradition. David Kinsley explains that "for millions of her devotees her power, influence, and grace have overflowed the categories that would restrict her to a subordinate, peripheral role."

Mary's popularity continues to grow. An especially intriguing manifestation of this is the interest in Black Madonnas. Their very darkness sets them apart from traditional lighter-than-air images of Mary. The Black Madonnas of France, Spain, and Switzerland convey a sense of weight, of substance, of being-in-matter. By implication they reclaim the earthy qualities of the feminine so long rejected by Western culture. Modern pilgrims report being deeply moved in the presence of Black Madonnas. Clearly, for those in the West, they fulfill a deep need for the sacred feminine.

Mary Magdalene represents another aspect of the sacred feminine in Christianity. Traditionally portrayed as a prostitute, Mary Magdalene is gaining respect among those challenging the suppression of women's contributions to the early Christian church. Gospels, especially those outside the ones selected for inclusion in today's Bible, point to Mary Magdalene's special relationship with Jesus. Mary Magdalene is viewed as a mortal woman, a sexual being, and a devoted follower—perhaps even the preeminent devotee—of Jesus.

Some surmise that Mary Magdalene was the spouse of Jesus. One popular writer portrays her as the mother of Jesus' child, and suggests that she is the true Holy Grail, the sacred chalice of the Divine. The suggestion that a woman might well have been an important disciple of Jesus challenges the traditional view that power and privilege in the church are reserved for men only. It seems that the interest in Mary Magdalene reflects the growing presence of spiritual feminism in Christianity.

Sacred Feminine West and East

European and Indian Goddess traditions share common sources and mutual influences. One example is Danu (also known as Don or Dana), the primordial water goddess of Irish and Welsh mythology. The Danaan people who introduced her to the West seem to have migrated from areas near the Aegean Sea bordering modern-day Turkey. They appear in Irish legend as the Tuatha de Danaan, "the folk of the god whose mother is Danu." They were apparently uprooted and migrated widely, leaving place names that mark their passing. Scholars theorize that their movements north and west are associated with the naming of the river Don in Russia, the Danube River in Europe, and perhaps even the country of the Danes, or Denmark.

The Danaan people may have assimilated into eastern and southern regions as well. The similarities between Danu and the Indian goddess Ganga are given as evidence. Both are goddesses of water, especially the flowing water of rivers. The sacred river Ganges is the namesake of the goddess Ganga. Pilgrims who bathe in her waters are absolved of all their sins, and those who die on her banks go directly to a divine afterlife.

It is thought that people traveled trade routes from Mesopotamia in the Middle East, bringing their goddess religions with them to the Indian subcontinent, where they blended with indigenous cultures. Scholars suggest that the idea of the sacred, centered space that is the essence of the mandala originated in what is now Iraq. Here, along the riverbanks, ancient peoples made stepped mounds, or ziggurats. Often crowned by a tree, these were sacred places for goddess worship. Careful observations of the movement of heavenly bodies were made from atop these ziggurats, as planets were thought to be goddesses. For example, the goddess Inanna was described as the morning and evening star, or the planet Venus.

The idea of sacred, centered space may have traveled from Middle Eastern lands, or it may have spontaneously emerged in India. Any resemblance to practices elsewhere can be explained by Jung's idea that human beings share universal ways of structuring their experiences, resulting in similarities that transcend cultural differences. This is demonstrated by the fact that mandalas can be seen not only in India but also in the arabesque patterns of Islamic art, the meandering designs of Celtic art, the sand paintings of Navajo Indians (figure 5), and the expressive art of Western psychotherapy patients (figure 6). Whether the appearance of mandalas in India is the result of cultural influences or of deeply ingrained human traits, the study of Indian tra-

ditions of the sacred feminine can show us possibilities we may not have envisioned. Those of us in the West can claim the sacred circles of India as our heritage, too.

The Sacred Feminine in India

The Goddess was also suppressed in India, but, with the passage of time, she resurfaced just as powerful as before. Paradoxically, the relegation of Goddess worship to lesser importance actually served to preserve it. In northern India beginning around 1750 B.C.E., the patriarchal Aryan culture confronted the matriarchal Harappans. The Aryans imposed their male-dominated religion in cities where women were not allowed to take part in the most respected rituals. Village life went on much as before, so women simply continued the old goddess traditions unnoticed. Passed from mother to daughter, the old spells, chants,

FIGURE 6

Modern psychotherapy clients create mandalas reminiscent of ancient imagery. In this mandala, a woman contemplates a precious egg, suggesting the balancing of masculine and feminine energies in the psyche. Based on a drawing by one of Jung's patients. (After Jung, 1959, 1969, fig. 24)

and magical diagrams, or *yantras,* were relied upon to ensure fertility, protect against the evil eye, and bring family prosperity.

Images of the Goddess reflected her presence as matter and the natural forces that animate and shape it. The Goddess religion in India became increasingly complex as the worship traditions of villagers merged with the transcendental visions of poets, mystics, and artists. Poetry, music, dance, and ritual art forms—including mandalas—have evolved as expressions of devotion to the Goddess. The ancient Goddess is again preeminent in the religious traditions of India; Suzanne Ironbiter observes that "her forms embody the cyclical rhythms of birth, life, and death that underlie the evolution and development of consciousness."

In one of her more archaic forms, the Goddess is associated in every possible way with the lotus blossom. Heinrich Zimmer cites descriptions of her as "lotus-born," "standing on a lotus," "lotus-colored," "lotus-thighed," "lotus-eyed," "decked with lotus garlands," and "abounding in lotuses." Among her many names are Padma and Kamala, both meaning "lotus." The lotus signifies the presence of the ancient Great Mother Goddess even when she is not named, as we see in Zimmer's recounting of a Hindu creation story:

> When the divine life substance is about to put forth the universe, the cosmic waters grow a thousand-petaled lotus of pure gold, radiant as the sun. This is the door or gate, the opening or mouth, of the womb of the universe. It is the first product of the creative principle, gold in token of its incorruptible nature. It opens to give birth first to the creator Brahma. From its pericarp [seed vessel] then issue the hosts of the created world.

In this myth the waters, too, are feminine. As Zimmer explains, "They are the maternal, procreative aspect of the Absolute, and the cosmic lotus is their generative organ." This sublime birth imagery links the sacred circle of the mandala with the lotus and therefore with the generative womb of the Great Goddess. The cosmic lotus is called the "highest form or aspect of Earth," "Goddess Moisture,"

and "Goddess Earth." It is personified as the Mother Goddess, through whom the Absolute moves into creation. Two of her classic names are Shri and Lakshmi.

The goddess Lakshmi has been known and worshiped from the earliest times. One of the most popular goddesses in the Hindu pantheon, she is often hailed as Shri Lakshmi. *Shri* is an honorific used in early Vedic hymns to suggest beauty, radiance, and nobility. The goddess is also a source of ruling authority. Lakshmi is revered as the source of wealth, abundance, and worldly success. She is richly dressed and shines with the radiance of sun, moon, and fire.

Lakshmi is also associated with fertility. She is described as moist, perceptible through odor, abundant in harvest, and dwelling in cow dung. As the lotus is rooted in the mud beneath still waters, so Lakshmi is associated with the rich, nourishing muck that sustains life. This earthy aspect of Lakshmi is especially important in rural areas where village women are known to sculpt small mounds of cow dung to represent the goddess during seasonal festivities. As Kinsley explains:

> The goddess Shri-Lakshmi represents the fully developed blossoming of organic life—indeed she might be taken as a symbol of the entire created world, the growing, expanding world imbued with vigorous fertile power. Shri-Lakshmi is the nectar or essence of creation that lends to creation its distinctive flavor and beauty. Organic life, impelled as it is by this mysterious power flowers richly and beautifully in the creative processes of the world.

The lotus of Lakshmi also conveys the attainment of spiritual power. The lotus seat is a common motif in both Hindu and Buddhist iconography. The gods and goddesses, the buddhas and bodhisattvas, typically sit or stand upon a lotus that signifies their spiritual authority (see mandala 43). Their lotus seat suggests that they have transcended the limitations of the finite world (the mud) to blossom freely in a full expression of human potential for spiritual realization. Kinsley concludes, "Shri-Lakshmi, then, suggests more than the fertilizing powers of moist soil and the mysterious powers of growth. She suggests perfection or a state of refinement that transcends the material world."

Mandalas and Yantras of the Sacred Feminine

A shrine (c. 10,000–8,000 B.C.E.) discovered by archeologists in India shows the venerable tradition of sacred circles in Goddess worship. The shrine's circular platform of sandstone supports pieces of striated rock. Nearby pieces, fitted together with matching elements on the platform, form a triangle of stone in shades of red. The use of such abstract symbols to convey the living presence of the Goddess continues today throughout India.

In parallel with the worship of the Goddess in these concrete manifestations, Indian mystics cultivated direct experiences of the Absolute, the One, through meditation. Through these experiences their view of reality and the nature of the self were transformed, and they became enlightened. Some of these gifted men and women created circular mandala drawings as an expression of their experiences and as maps of inner reality. These mandalas were used as a visual aid to return, at will, to enlightened states of consciousness, and they were also useful for training others in the skill. Mandalas evolved as symbols, invocations, and containers of transpersonal energies. As objects of meditation, they act to protect the psychic space and concentration of the practitioner.

Mandalas are circles that create a sacred space. In Eastern traditions, they are also maps of the cosmos, delineating the process by which things are created and come into being—then cease to be, reabsorbed into the All. These ceaseless activities are thought to revolve around a central axis that is symbolized by the center point of the mandala. Sometimes the center of the mandala is occupied by a mythic mountain that supports the sky and rests upon a mystery beyond knowing. In other mandalas, the throne or dwelling place of a deity rests upon the sacred center. In both examples, the process by which the cosmos comes into being is understood as symbolic of the path to mystical states of consciousness.

Mandalas often incorporate an outer square that represents a protective enclosure, with four gates facing the four cardinal directions. It clearly separates the sacred inner space of the mandala from the unsanctified outer area. Lotus petals are arranged around the inner circle, alluding to the primordial lotus goddess as the doorway of creation. The lotus also signifies the aspiration to transcend ordinary existence.

An image of the Goddess in human form may be placed in the center of a mandala. She may also be represented by a sacred word or letter that expresses her essence. Her presence may even be conveyed by a geometric design known as a *yantra*. An important feature is the nodal point at the center, the *bindu*. Represented by a small dot or circle, the bindu allows the primal feminine energy, personified as the goddess Shakti, to enter the design. With the presence of Shakti, the creation becomes alive.

(In drawing the mandalas for this book, I experienced the transformation of a circular design when the center point is inked in place. Instantly the eyes begin tracing all sorts of patterns that went unnoticed before the center point was clearly established. Pulsating figure/ground relationships dance into being. The importance of the bindu must come, to some degree, from this visual effect. Perhaps you will notice this too when you draw some of the mandalas in the back of this book.)

Yantras are part of the Hindu tradition, while mandalas appear in both Hindu and Buddhist art. In practice, a distinction between yantras and mandalas is difficult to make. Even experts such as Giuseppe Tucci view them as very similar. "The yantra does not differ from the mandala. The meaning and use of both are the same."

Disciplines for creating mandalas and yantras are traditionally transmitted as sacred practices from spiritual teacher to student. Strict rules govern the time, place, and technical aspects of the formation of these designs. *Mantras*—voiced sounds that express and invoke sacred energies—are intoned to generate the proper state of mind for creating particular designs and to imbue them with the essence of the Goddess, whose presence is ritually invited by creating the design. The mandala or yantra may be utilized for meditation, folded into an amulet and worn, or ritually destroyed when the special occasion for which they are created comes to a conclusion.

Tantric Symbolism in Mandalas

Mandalas are especially important in Hindu tantrism, which envisions the cosmos as comprised of complementary forces symbolized by the female Shakti and the male Shiva. Shakti is primordial energy, envisioned as the creative force that quickens and sets in motion the rhythms of life. Shiva is thought of as cosmic consciousness, the essential ground of all phenomena. As Madhav Khanna explains, "Śiva is the silent seer of all phenomena, the innermost point of the subjective self (consciousness) and Śakti is the phenomenon itself (matter)." In the tantric view, all that exists flows from the creative play between these two forces.

Although Shiva and Shakti appear to be in opposition, in reality they are perfectly balanced aspects of transcendent wholeness. They are eternally inseparable. Each must have the other in order to manifest its full potential. A sacred text states: "Just as moonbeams cannot be separated from the moon nor the rays from the sun, so Shakti cannot be distinguished from Shiva." Shiva is sometimes symbolized in sacred images as Shiva-bindu, a single point representing the latent potential for creation. Around the center point of the Shiva-bindu lies Shakti in the form of a *chakra,* or "wheel." "This is the primal form of the mandala," states Jung. (This chakra is also called a *padma,* or lotus, alluding to the presence of the archaic lotus goddess mentioned earlier.)

Tantrism sees the cosmic duality of Shiva-Shakti reflected in the microcosm of the human body and the subtle energies that flow within it. Shakti energy manifests in the body as Kundalini and nestles at the base of the spine. Shakti-Kundalini energy flows from the base of the spine upward through the two psychic nerve pathways of the subtle body. As energy moves through the chakras, or nodal points where the nerves cross, Shakti and Shiva unite in configurations of increasing refinement until their final union in the highest chakra, the *sahasrara* chakra. Located at the crown of the head, this is the highest spiritual center and the seat of Shiva. (Plate 5 portrays mandalas that represent the chakras.)

The great Shri Yantra is ancient (see plate 9 and mandala 41). The earliest surviving Shri Yantra is preserved in a religious institution established in the eighth century C.E.,

though the design is no doubt much older. A description of a similar geometric form is found in the *Atharva Veda* (c. 1200 B.C.E.). The yantra contains layer upon layer of sacred significance. Its name proclaims an association with the omnipresent Lotus Goddess, Shri Lakshmi.

In the Shri Yantra we find a spectacular example of the dynamic play of Shiva and Shakti. Since Shiva and Shakti are inseparable, all yantras dedicated to goddesses (because they are emanations of Shakti) imply Shiva qualities as well. Downward-pointing triangles signify Shakti energy. Upward-pointing triangles represent the quiescent potential of Shiva. The interpenetration of the triangles symbolizes the creation of the cosmos when these two forces come together.

The Shri Yantra is also a graphic metaphor of life and the attainment of spiritual realization. It represents all that is, as well as the pathway to transcending the world of the senses. The Shri Yantra depicts a spiritual journey that moves through nine stages. At each stage the aspirant advances toward the center, where he or she experiences the unity of all existence. The nine stages of the journey are represented by nine concentric circles that underlie the structure of the Shri Yantra.

Starting from the outer square and moving inward, the realizations to be attained at each stage are personified by groupings of goddesses. All the goddesses are understood to emanate from Shakti, who resides at the center point, or bindu, sheathed in the form of the goddess Lalita (pure consciousness). The spun-off goddesses comprise "Shakti clusters." Each group of goddesses reveals the wisdom to be attained at that stage of the journey.

As the devotee focuses attention on the yantra, moving from the outer to the inner rings, more and more refined states of consciousness are experienced. One stage helps the aspirant master natural human egotism, while another supports the mastery of nonattachment to the information from the senses that veils spiritual insight. Yet another promotes awareness of the vital energies of the subtle body. With proficiency, the aspirant is able to penetrate to the center—the bindu—where all the Shakti clusters dissolve into pure consciousness with the realization that there is only One, the All, the Absolute.

The pathway to realization symbolized by the Shri Yantra is one of gradual development. Real life is seldom orderly, and Indian goddesses embody the darkness and chaos of life as well as the light and order. So it is that one of the most important goddesses in the Hindu pantheon is Kali, the Dark One. Kali encompasses within herself the powers of both creation and destruction. She is the symbol of the unstoppable passage of time, and of the dynamism of creation. Thomas Cleary and Aziz Sartaz state the paradox that underlies Kali's essence as the mistress of time: "Time is movement; movement enlivens. Time is also transitoriness; transitoriness kills." Kali's powerful presence is evoked in Jayakar's poetic description of a bronze figure crafted by a village artisan:

> The devouring goddess, black as the dark night, is depicted with a skull-like face, shrilly gaping mouth, and round, prominent bulging eyes. The hair is drawn off the face and tied in a pigtail. The body of the goddess, cast as a thin plaque of metal, is angled to delineate the waist. The breasts are immature, for she is a virgin. She wears no ornaments save for a girdle around her waist. The goddess is four-armed. The savagely lean and gaunt image, open-mouthed, devourer of him who devours [Shiva], strikes and pierces the heart of the worshipper. The urgent demand for protection, a wild piercing cry, is held in the face of the dark Mother. It is the poignancy of this fear that creates Kali. She is conceived of terror, drinks the terror deep, darkens with it, till she is the color of "kalaratri," the darkest moonless night. Then she devours terror, annihilates it, cleaving through the darkness of terror. Then arising, emerging to sustain and protect, her wild mask of terror is transmuted to the face adorable as the image of all tenderness.

Kali's Ten Wisdoms

Kali is thought of as the mother or matrix of the Shakti cluster known as the Dasha Mahavidyas (Ten Transcendent

Wisdoms). An ancient story explains how she came to hold her supreme power over all of existence.

Shiva, the god of destruction, he of the unchanging, masculine principle, was quarreling with Sati (the previous incarnation of his consort, the goddess Parvati). Suddenly, the goddess Kali emerged as a manifestation of Shiva's consort and confronted Shiva. He turned and ran away from her, but Kali instantly generated an image of herself in front of him and blocked his escape. He then turned and ran in a different direction, and again Kali placed an aspect of herself before him and blocked his way. Again and again he turned a different way to escape the goddess, but each time she was there in a different form. After his escape was stymied at every turn by Kali, Shiva was forced to acknowledge that she was more powerful than he.

As Khanna explains, "Kali 'filled' the four quarters, in ten directions, with her ten energies, which are to her what sparks are to fire." Kali's ten energies, or wisdoms, are personified in the Ten Mahavidyas (see plate 11). The Mahavidyas are understood to represent the experiences that comprise the human condition. This explains their designation as transcendent wisdom. According to Khanna, "together, they are the expression of the cycles of life, and the summary of all planes of existence. They represent forces that are related to the powers of time, of death, of the continuous flux of life which is a constant reminder that life is a passing phenomenon."

Each of the ten manifestations is a goddess in her own right. Each has a specific cosmic function, and each has her rituals, mantra, and yantra. (The yantras of the Ten Mahavidyas are included in the coloring section, mandalas 16–25.) From the circumstances of one's life, the goddess who is present, or who could be helpful, can be identified and propitiated for a desirable outcome. Chanting her mantra and creating the yantra invite her energies.

The yantras of the Ten Mahavidyas are sometimes presented in a circle—a sort of mandala of yantras—that emphasizes the cyclical nature of the totality that they represent (figure 7). Like a turning wheel of fortune, the conditions represented by the goddesses follow in a logical order from positive to negative, and back again to positive. Envisioning the yantras superimposed on the face of a

FIGURE 7

Yantras of the Ten Mahavidyas, goddesses who manifest aspects of Kali (center yantra). From the top clockwise: Kali, Tara, Shodashi, Bhuvaneshvari, Chinnamasta, Bhairavi, Dhumavati, Bagalamukhi, Matangi, Kamala. (After Khanna, p. 59)

clock, Kali occupies the high-noon position. The other goddesses (who are also aspects of Kali) take their positions in a clockwise fashion beginning with Tara, then Shodashi, Bhuvaneshvari, Chinnamasta, Tripura Bhairavi, Dhumavati, Bagalamukhi, Matangi, and Kamala. As the first of the Mahavidyas, Kali is worshipped for knowledge of the inexorable force of time unfolding in the existence of the universe, or the transitoriness of all things.

The second Mahavidya, Tara ("savioress"), is thought to have originated as a Buddhist deity (see plate 4). She symbolizes the possibility of triumphing over time-bound human existence with eternal spiritual life, and so provides inspiration and assistance to those who engage in the process of personal transformation. Her yantra is an eight-petaled lotus in a circle, with an inverted triangle, pointing

toward the goddess's fundamental quality—the pure desire to create.

The third Mahavidya, Shodashi, represents the power of perfection and sustenance. Her name, meaning "one who is sixteen," is associated with totality in Hindu tradition. Shodashi represents the fulfillment of the creative cycle, when the entire universe, like a flower, is in full bloom. This quality is represented in her yantra with its nine triangles thought of as cosmic wombs. She is invoked either in the great Shri Yantra or in her own yantra.

The fourth goddess is Bhuvaneshvari ("queen of the world"). She is radiant and beautiful. Bhuvaneshvari is associated with the earth. Her epithets, "Form of Everything" and "All-Containing Form," point to her as the one who sets things in order. She serves both constructive and conservative purposes. Bhuvaneshvari teaches that order, although beneficial, can stultify existence if it is clung to as an end in itself. She appears in her yantra seated on a hexagon of two superimposed triangles, which are emblematic of the synergy of the two principles—male and female—as one.

The fifth Mahavidya is Chinnamasta ("decapitated"). She is shown holding her head in her left hand while drinking streams of blood-nectar flowing from her own severed neck. Some believe this iconography represents the rising of Kundalini energy up the channels of the subtle body. It might also refer to the necessity of sacrifice in sustaining life. As Cleary and Aziz explain, "Just as the goddess's head also drinks her blood, so is earth's fertility renewed by death, much as a tree is fertilized by the decay of its own fallen leaves." In her yantra, the destructive aspect of her image is implied symbolically by triangles and circles.

Bhairavi ("terrible one"), the sixth manifestation, is the destructive power of Kali. Bhairavi embodies the inexorable force of dissolution that commences at the very moment something comes into being. In the Hindu view of reality, the two opposing forces of growth and decay permeate all existence. Her yantra is a hexagon placed within a circle of lotuses. The annihilating power of time is represented in the yantra of this goddess by the nine triangles that symbolize the disintegration of existence.

The seventh Mahavidya, Dhumavati ("smoky one"), is the antithesis of the goddess as moist and life-sustaining. She appears as an old widow without mercy for those who suffer. Dhumavati embodies ultimate destruction, capable of reducing the world to ashes. She signifies misfortune of all kinds. When the universe is inert, sleeping, dead, Dhumavati brings on the cosmic darkness—a necessary stage in the cosmic cycles. She encourages a turning away from the world. Dhumavati's yantra is a hexagon within an eight-petaled lotus.

Bagalamukhi ("face to the side") is the eighth manifestation of Kali. She is a crane-headed goddess invoked for magical powers that put a stop to any actions or impulses. Her help is sought to cool a hot temperament and to halt dangerous storms and other forms of destruction. Her yantra is like Dhumavati's except for an additional triangle inside the hexagon.

The ninth Mahavidya, Matangi ("intoxicated limbs"), embodies the truth that the goddess is the ultimate outsider, beyond the class or caste distinctions of human society. In Hinduism, Matangi is considered an outcast goddess for those who are untouchable by traditional cultural standards. Matangi banishes evil, metes out justice, and grants psychic powers, wealth, and literary ability as well as protection from evil spirits. Her yantra is the same as Dhumavati's.

The tenth Mahavidya is Kamala ("lotus"). In her, we find the benevolent and wish-fulfilling aspect of Kali. Kamala is like a flower blossoming in everything and represents a state of renewal following the previous stages of darkness and destruction. She is the embodiment of all that is desirable, and reveals herself in everything that brings one joy and fulfillment. Cleary and Aziz call her "identical with creation, with the cause of creation, and with supreme spiritual bliss." Interestingly, the yantra of the creative Kamala, a hexagon within a circle of lotuses, is very similar to that of the destructive Dhumavati.

The Ten Mahavidyas represent the great round of human existence in its light and dark aspects. The wisdom of these goddesses addresses the cyclical ups and downs of life. All human experiences are within their purview. The Shakti cluster of the Mahavidyas reflects the Indian view

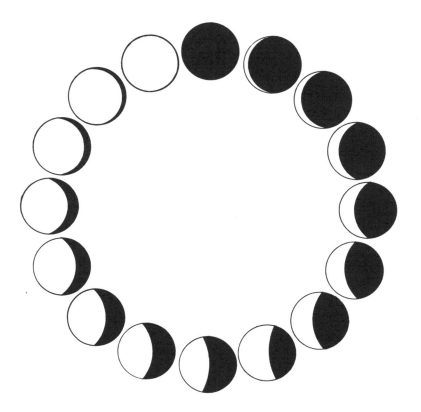

FIGURE 8

Nitya Shaktis (moon goddesses) are associated with moon phases. Clockwise, beginning from the dark new moon, goddesses one by one add to the brilliance of the moon with their presence.

that existence is a dynamic unity, and all of life—the dark and the light, the dynamic and the static—are necessary parts of the whole.

Moon Goddesses of Delight

Another Shakti cluster, the sixteen Nitya Shaktis (moon goddesses), are worshiped in lunar phases (see figure 8). Fifteen Nityas represent bright phases of the moon. A tantric text proclaims, "The fifteen Nityas represent the fifteen lunar days and the lunar days are the union of Shiva-Shakti." The sixteenth Nitya resides in the dark stage of the moon. A charming story explains that when the moon is full, all fifteen light Nityas are present, causing the moon to shine brightly. One by one the Nityas leave the moon and go to the sun, reducing the moon in size. By the sixteenth phase, the moon is completely dark. Then the Nityas begin returning to the moon, one by one, until the cycle is completed when the moon is full again.

The goddess Lalita, whose nature is pure consciousness, is the source of both light and dark Nityas. Hindu scripture describes the sixteen Nityas as the limbs or rays of Lalita. The waxing and waning moon is a constant reminder that life swells with increase, recedes, disappears, and is reborn in ever-repeating, predictable rhythms. The Nityas are also identified with the rhythms of breath and with the continuum of consciousness, from deep sleep to dreaming, waking, and full consciousness. Khanna observes, "The circle of the Nitya Shaktis is a reservoir of delight, for they embody all those aspects of life that make existence a celebration of the spirit. They combine the all-beneficent aspects of the Divine. The worship of their yantras grants boons, dispels fear and brings enjoyment to the worshipper." (Yantras of the Nitya Shaktis are included in the coloring section, mandalas 26–41.)

The first Nitya Shakti in the cycle of the waxing moon is Kameshvari, who represents the dark before the new moon. She grants wishes. Bhagamalini arouses. Nityaklinna

grants supernatural powers. Bherunda clears evil influences. Vahnivasini, the fire-dweller, gives one mastery over the forces of nature. Mahavajresvari, the embodiment of mercy, does away with cruelty. Duti kills fear, brings prosperity, and grants one's desires. Tvarita ("swift") bestows beauty and fame and quickly expands the faculties of learning. Kulasundari ("beautiful heart") rewards with esoteric knowledge. Nitya-Nitya is beneficent. Nilapataka ("sapphire banner") gives one the power to control evil forces in nature. Vijaya stands for victories and prosperity. Sarvamangala ("all-auspicious") is totally benevolent. Jvalamalini ("garlanded with flame") gives spiritually beneficial knowledge of one's previous births. Chitra ("variegated") provides that which is desired and banishes fears. The sixteenth Nitya Shakti in the cycle of the waxing moon is Adya Nitya, who represents the full moon that absorbs the other fifteen Nityas. She is all-beneficent.

All the aspects of the Goddess represent the many transformations of one supreme consciousness in manifestation. They provide a way to relate to a reality that is hard to grasp, and help us appreciate the spiritual nature of ordinary existence. Our drawing and coloring mandalas of the sacred feminine is a meditation that can guide us toward becoming centered in this truth.

References

Anderson, Sherry Ruth, and Patricia Hopkins. *The Feminine Face of God: The Unfolding of the Sacred in Women*. New York: Bantam Books, 1992.

Argüelles, José, and Miriam Argüelles. *Mandala*. Boulder & London: Shambhala Publications, 1972.

Budapest, Zsuzsanna E. *The Grandmother of Time*. San Francisco: Harper & Row Publishers, 1989.

Campbell, Joseph. *Hero with a Thousand Faces*. New York: World Publishing Co., 1949.

Chicago, Judy. *Through the Flower: My Struggle as a Woman Artist*. Rev. ed. Garden City, N.Y.: Anchor Books, 1982.

Christ, Carol P. *Odyssey with the Goddess: A Spiritual Quest in Crete*. New York: Continuum, 1995.

———. *Rebirth of the Goddess: Finding Meaning in Feminist Spirituality*. New York & London: Routledge, 2004.

Cleary, Thomas, and Aziz Sartaz. *Twilight Goddess*. Boston: Shambhala Publications, 2000.

Clift, Jean Dalby, and Wallace B. Clift. *The Archetype of Pilgrimage*. New York: Paulist Press, 1996.

Cooper, J. C. *An Illustrated Encylopaedia of Traditional Symbols*. London: Thames & Hudson, 1978.

Craighead, Meinrad. *The Mother's Songs: Images of God the Mother*. New York: Paulist Press, 1986.

Curry, Nancy A., and Tim Kasser. "Can Coloring Mandalas Reduce Anxiety?" *Art Therapy: Journal of the American Art Therapy Association* 22, no. 2 (2005): 81–85.

Daly, Mary. *Beyond God the Father: Toward a Philosophy of Women's Liberation*. Boston: Beacon Press, 1973.

Fincher, Susanne F. *Coloring Mandalas*. Boston: Shambhala Publications, 2000.

———. *Creating Mandalas: For Insight, Healing, and Self-Expression*. Boston: Shambhala Publications, 1991.

———. *Menopause: The Inner Journey*. Boston: Shambhala Publications, 1995.

Fox, Matthew. *Creation Spirituality: Liberating Gifts for the Peoples of the Earth*. San Francisco: HarperSanFrancisco, 1991.

Frazer, James George. *The Golden Bough*. 1922. Reprint, New York: Macmillan Publishing Co., 1950.

Gimbutas, Marija. *The Language of the Goddess*. San Francisco: Harper & Row, 1989.

Ironbiter, Suzanne. *Devi*. Stamford, Conn.: Yuganta Press, 1987.

Jayakar, Pupul. *The Earth Mother: Legends, Ritual Arts, and Goddesses of India*. San Francisco: Harper & Row, 1990.

Jung, C. G. *Mandala Symbolism*. 1959. Translated by R. F. C. Hull. Reprint, Princeton, N.J.: Princeton University Press, 1969.

———. *The Psychology of Kundalini Yoga: Notes of the Seminar Given in 1932 by C. G. Jung*. Edited by Sonu Shamdasani. Princeton, N.J.: Princeton University Press, 1996.

Khanna, Madhu. *Yantra: The Tantric Symbol of Cosmic Unity*. London: Thames & Hudson, 1979.

King, Karen L. *The Gospel of Mary of Magdala: Jesus and the First Woman Disciple*. Santa Rosa, Calif.: Polebridge Press, 2003.

Kinsley, David. *Hindu Goddesses: Visions of the Divine Feminine in the Hindu Religious Tradition*. Berkeley, Calif.: University of California Press, 1986.

Klein, Jared. Personal communication with the author, December 11, 2005.

Matthews, Caitlin. *Mabon and the Mysteries of Britain: An Exploration of the Mabinogion*. London: Penguin Books, 1987.

Mookerjee, Ajit. *Tantra Art: Its Philosophy and Physics*. 1971. Reprint, Basel, Paris & New Delhi: Ravi Kumar, 1972.

Neumann, Erich. *The Great Mother*. 1955. Translated by Ralph Manheim. Reprint, Princeton, N.J.: Princeton University Press, 1963.

———. *The Origins and History of Consciousness*. Princeton, N.J.: Princeton University Press, 1954.

Pagels, Elaine. *Beyond Belief: The Secret Gospel of Thomas*. New York: Random House, 2003.

Spretnak, Charlene. *Lost Goddesses of Early Greece: A Collection of Pre-Hellenic Myths*. Boston: Beacon Press, 1978.

Starhawk. *The Spiral Dance: A Rebirth of the Ancient Religion of the Great Goddess*. 1979. Reprint, San Francisco: Harper & Row, 1989.

Stone, Merlin. *When God Was a Woman*. San Diego, Calif.: Harcourt Brace & Co., 1976.

Tucci, Giuseppe. *The Theory and Practice of the Mandala*. New York: Samuel Weiser, 1961.

Waters, Frank. *Masked Gods*. New York: Ballantine Books, 1975.

Wolkstein, Diane, and Samuel Noah Kramer. *Inanna: Queen of Heaven and Earth, Her Stories and Hymns from Sumer*. New York: Harper & Row, 1983.

Zimmer, Heinrich. *Myths and Symbols in Indian Art and Civilization*. Edited by Joseph Campbell. Princeton, N.J.: Princeton University Press, 1946.

PLATE 1
Master Healer Mandala
At the center is the goddess Prajnaparamita. She personifies transcendent wisdom, the source of all enlightenment. Seated on a throne supported by lions and surrounded by an elaborate backrest, she sits in lotus posture with the right leg crossed over the left. Her four hands represent love, compassion, joy, and equanimity—qualities required of any healer. A circle of eight Medicine Buddhas surrounds the goddess. The Buddha Shakyamuni is in the upper left among rows of lineage teachers. (Collection of Shelley & Donald Rubin, item #902)

PLATE 2
Inanna

Sumerian goddess of the morning and evening star. This mandala incorporates symbols of the qualities of the goddess. A lapis lazuli necklace of authority encircles her star. Three circles of rose petals frame the mandala, signifying Inanna's three realms of sky, earth, and underworld, as well as the maiden, mature woman, and dark sister aspects of the goddess. The downward-pointing triangle alludes to Inanna's sexuality as the source of Nature's abundance. (Susanne F. Fincher)

PLATE 3
Wheel of Life

Many hands touch to form a protective circle of support around creatures taking form. The Goddess is seen in the web of life and the mystic's experience that the cosmos is held within an ineffable matrix of love. (© Lee Lawson)

PLATE 4
Tara
*Tara is a female buddha associated with practices that heal, protect, and
extend life. Her left hand gestures, "Fear not," while her right conveys, "I
have what you need." (Collection of Rubin Museum of Art, item #65257)*

PLATE 5
Radiant Woman
Mandalas mark nodal points, or chakras, where psychic energy is transformed as it flows upward along pathways near the spine. At each chakra, a marriage of feminine Shakti-Kundalini energy and masculine Shiva energy takes place. This creates synergy so that the process can continue in the next chakra. A man exploring his inner feminine nature through creative self-expression produced this painting. He came to understand that what appear to be the masculine-feminine opposites are really projections of an underlying unity. (From Mandala *by José and Miriam Argüelles, © 1972. Reprinted by arrangement with Shambhala Publications, Inc., Boston, www.shambhala.com)*

PLATE 6
Shri Devi

The circular diagram in the belly of the blue Glorious Goddess is in the form of a lotus, recalling the primordial Lotus Goddess, Shri. The design is a yantra with a black center, four red petals, and an outer ring edged with flames. The yantra is inscribed with verses, some for protection, others for the misfortune of enemies. This Tibetan painting was probably created to counter a perceived threat. (Collection of Rubin Museum of Art, item #65172)

PLATE 7
"Primordial Goddess" Plate, from *The Dinner Party*

The artist Judy Chicago used the traditionally feminine arts of china painting and embroidery to create a symbolic dinner party that traces the history of women in Western civilization. Ms. Chicago represents the sacred feminine in an image of interior, centered space surrounded by folds or undulations, as in the structure of the vagina, and uses this iconography to state the truth and beauty of her own identity as a woman. After centuries of neglect, the Goddess takes an honored place at the table. (© Judy Chicago, 1979)

PLATE 8

Death

The mystery of the sacred feminine as both womb and tomb means that death is seen as a central opening, a pathway of return to the welcoming darkness. (© Meinrad Craighead)

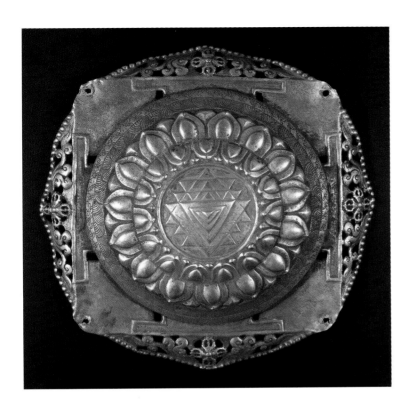

PLATE 9
Shri Yantra Mandala

The Shri Yantra is considered the greatest of all yantras. It is also one of the oldest with an early version described in the Atharva Veda (c. 1200 B.C.E.). The interpenetrating triangles are associated with masculine (Shiva) and feminine (Shakti) energies. The Shri Yantra represents the reality that the cosmos is an everlasting unity encompassing the creative tension of opposites. Bronze, Nepal, 19th century. (Collection of Shelley and Donald Rubin, item #700053)

PLATE 10
Nairatmya

The female buddha Nairatmya, "The Selfless One," is the focus of meditation practices introduced by Virupa, an 11th-century Indian adept. Tradition says that Virupa was initiated by Nairatmya herself in a series of disturbing dreams. The downward-pointing triangle represents her powerful feminine presence. Tibet, 17th century. (Collection of Rubin Museum of Art, item #643)

PLATE 11

Ten Mahavidyas

These ten goddesses manifest Kali's presence in all phases of existence, from delightful to horrific. Below each goddess is her yantra. This contemporary painting of traditional forms was created by a husband and wife team of tantric artists from Bihar in eastern India. Top row from left: Kali, Tara, Shodashi, Bhuvaneshvari, and Bhairavi. Bottom row from left: Chinnamasta, Dhumavati, Bagalamukhi, Matangi, and Kamala. (Poonam Devi and Basudev Jha, from the collection of Susanne F. Fincher)

Mandalas for Coloring

MANDALA 1
Tri-lines emphasize seed shapes that suggest the fecundity of the Goddess. Based on the design of a painted ceramic bowl. Spain, 3700–3500 B.C.E.

MANDALA 2

Crescent moon shapes alternate with tri-lines, imparting the energy of the Goddess as life force. Inspired by a painted ceramic platter. Bulgaria, 4500–4300 B.C.E.

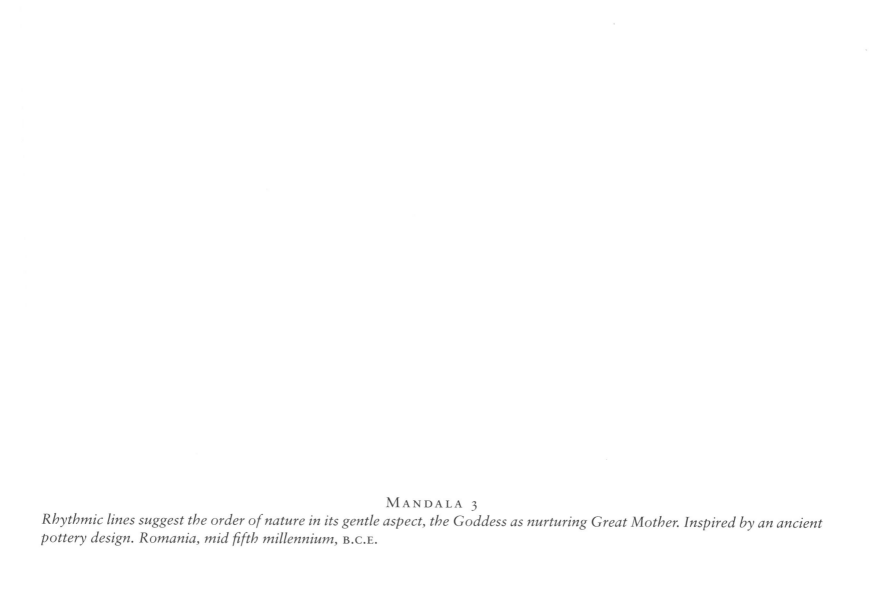

MANDALA 3

Rhythmic lines suggest the order of nature in its gentle aspect, the Goddess as nurturing Great Mother. Inspired by an ancient pottery design. Romania, mid fifth millennium, B.C.E.

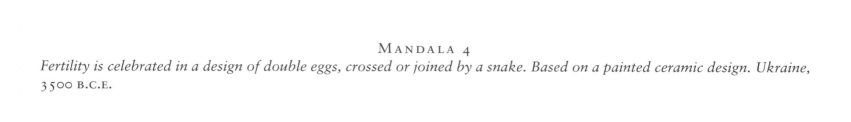

MANDALA 4
Fertility is celebrated in a design of double eggs, crossed or joined by a snake. Based on a painted ceramic design. Ukraine,
3500 B.C.E.

MANDALA 5
Tadpole shapes suggest the generativity of the Goddess. Inspired by a ceramic dish. Malta, c. 3000 B.C.E.

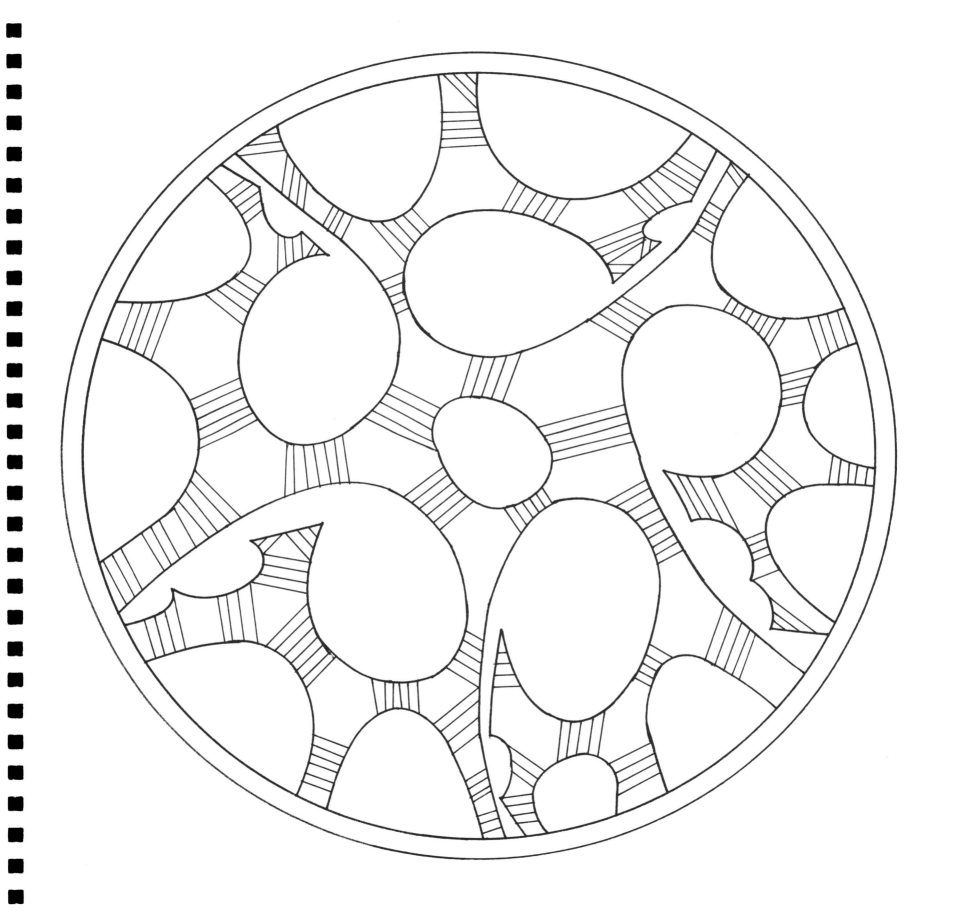

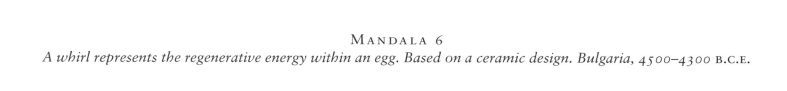

MANDALA 6
A whirl represents the regenerative energy within an egg. Based on a ceramic design. Bulgaria, 4500–4300 B.C.E.

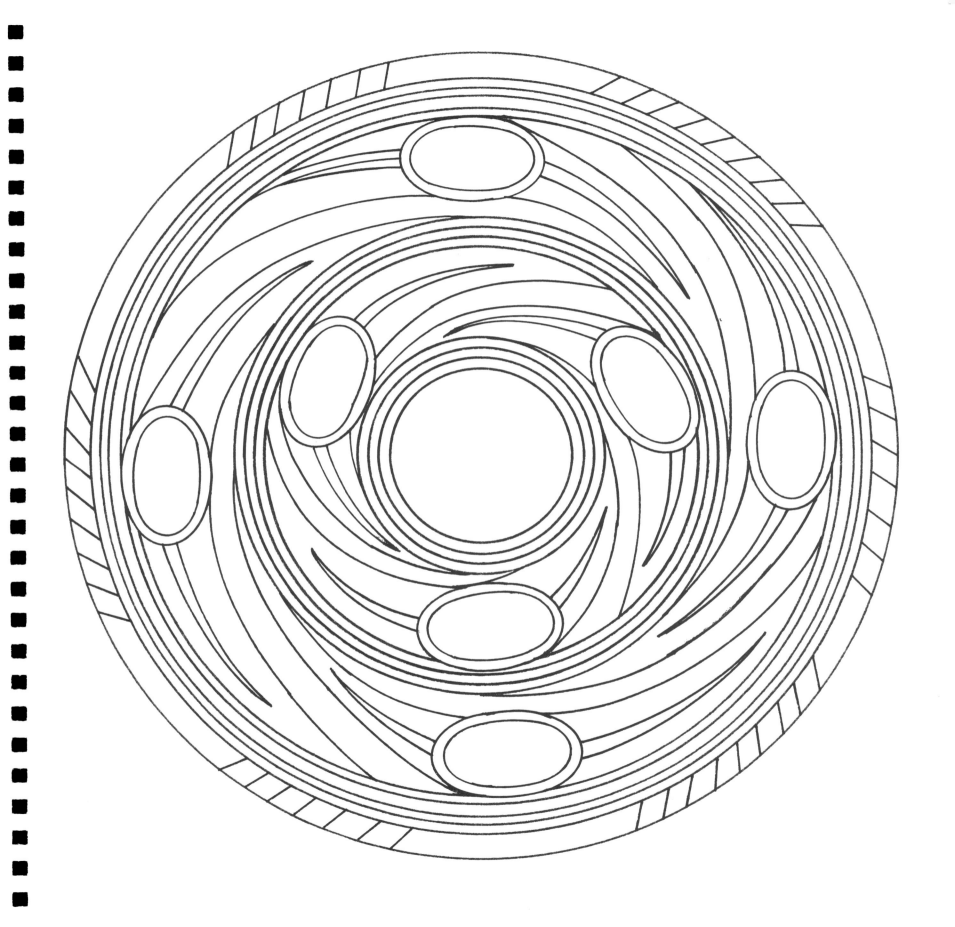

MANDALA 7

Her animals accompany the Goddess. The fish signifies her womb as the eternal source of life. The four-armed crosses are ancient auspicious symbols of the "sun wheel." Based on the design of an egg-shaped amphora found in a tomb. Greece, 700–675 B.C.E.

MANDALA 8

The Goddess is shown as a woman with the head of an insect. Winged hounds flank her. Double bull horns above her head suggest phases of the moon. Based on an onyx gem. Knossos, Crete, c. 1500 B.C.E.

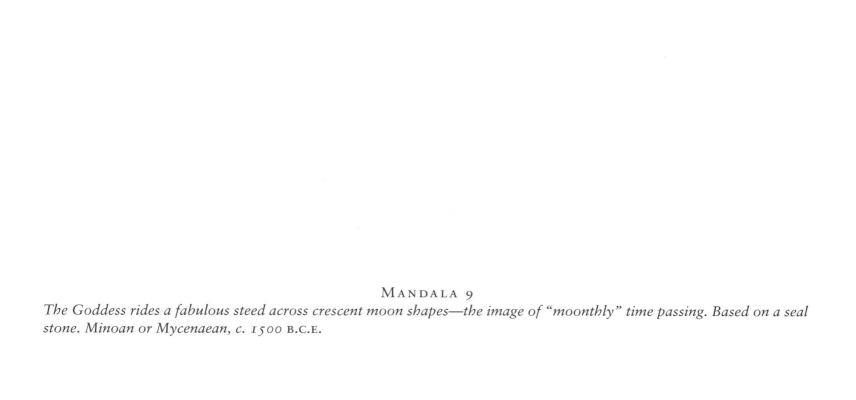

MANDALA 9

The Goddess rides a fabulous steed across crescent moon shapes—the image of "moonthly" time passing. Based on a seal stone. Minoan or Mycenaean, c. 1500 B.C.E.

MANDALA 10

The Goddess receives worship and gives abundance in this mandala design based on a gold seal ring. Minoan or Mycenaean, c. 1500 B.C.E.

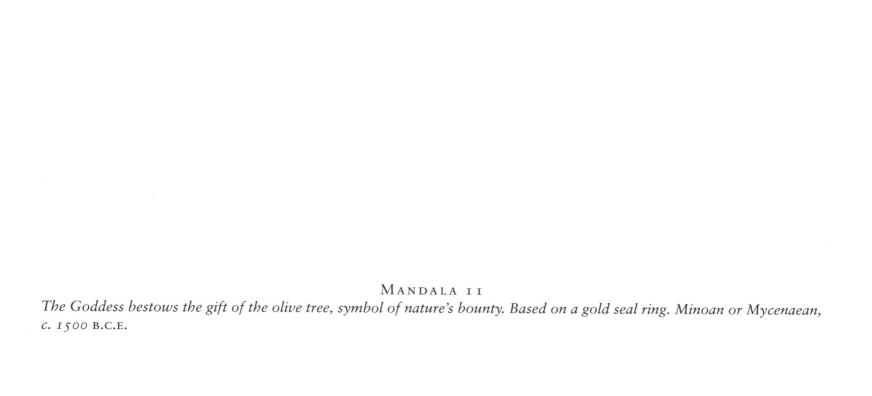

MANDALA 11

The Goddess bestows the gift of the olive tree, symbol of nature's bounty. Based on a gold seal ring. Minoan or Mycenaean, c. 1500 B.C.E.

MANDALA 12
A feathery fan suggests the eternal spinning of the wheel of time, or the blooming of a fabulous flower.

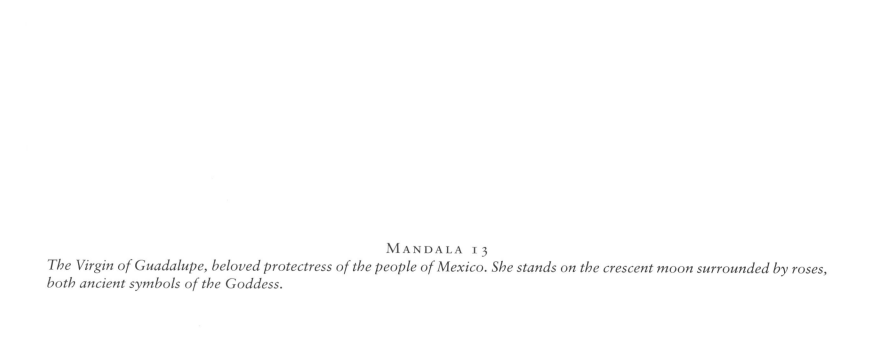

MANDALA 13

The Virgin of Guadalupe, beloved protectress of the people of Mexico. She stands on the crescent moon surrounded by roses, both ancient symbols of the Goddess.

MANDALA 14

Mother of God of the Myrtle Tree. *The Virgin takes residence in the myrtle tree, once sacred to Cretan Aphrodite. Christian worship merges with older forms of veneration of the sacred feminine.*

MANDALA 15

Shakti is the female energy that spins the world into being. Color this mandala from the center out and you will manifest a starflower. In this activity you are like the creative goddess Shakti, transforming kinesthetic movement into color and form.

MANDALA 16

Kali Yantra *(first of the Ten Mahavidyas). Kali is the supreme goddess of time, presiding over the present moment that gives life its vitality and its transitory nature as well.*

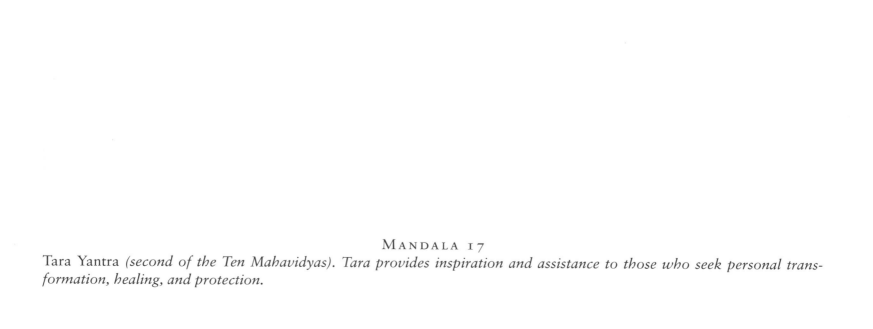

MANDALA 17

Tara Yantra *(second of the Ten Mahavidyas). Tara provides inspiration and assistance to those who seek personal transformation, healing, and protection.*

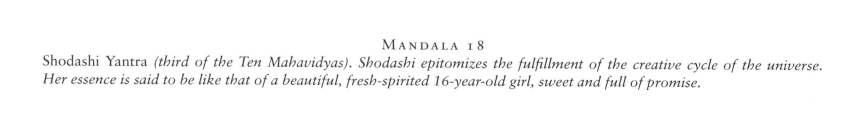

MANDALA 18

Shodashi Yantra *(third of the Ten Mahavidyas). Shodashi epitomizes the fulfillment of the creative cycle of the universe. Her essence is said to be like that of a beautiful, fresh-spirited 16-year-old girl, sweet and full of promise.*

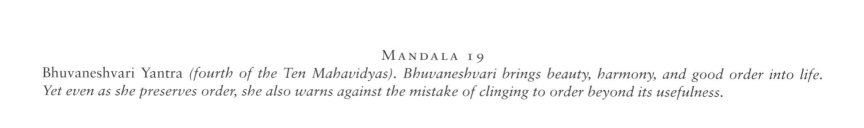

MANDALA 19

Bhuvaneshvari Yantra *(fourth of the Ten Mahavidyas). Bhuvaneshvari brings beauty, harmony, and good order into life. Yet even as she preserves order, she also warns against the mistake of clinging to order beyond its usefulness.*

MANDALA 20

Chinnamasta Yantra *(fifth of the Ten Mahavidyas). Chinnamasta symbolizes the positive effects of self-sacrifice. She reminds us that sometimes it is good to "lose your head," to let go of self-conscious thinking.*

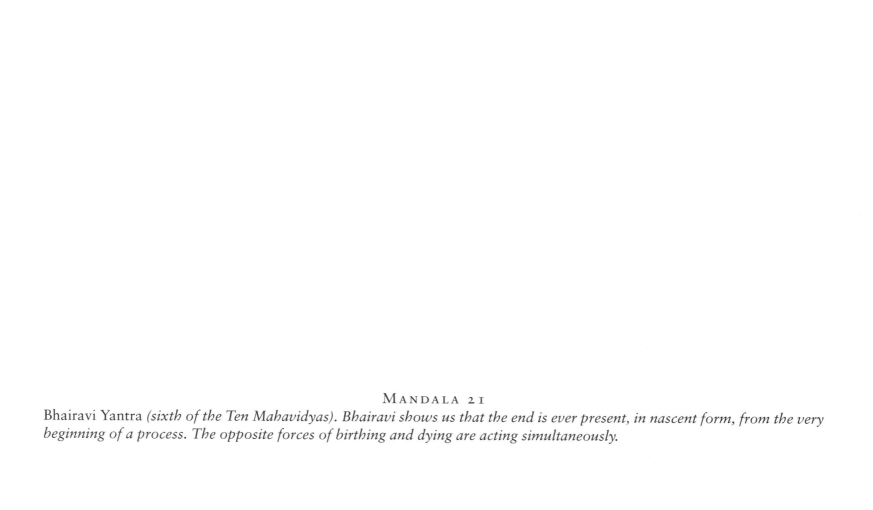

MANDALA 21

Bhairavi Yantra *(sixth of the Ten Mahavidyas). Bhairavi shows us that the end is ever present, in nascent form, from the very beginning of a process. The opposite forces of birthing and dying are acting simultaneously.*

MANDALA 22

Dhumavati Yantra *(seventh of the Ten Mahavidyas). Dhumavati is associated with misfortune of all kinds. She brings on the darkness that must precede any process of renewal. Under her influence, we are encouraged to turn away from worldly pursuits and look inward.*

Bagalamukhi Yantra *(eighth of the Ten Mahavidyas). Propitiating Bagalamukhi gains her help in cooling a hot temper, dissipating storms and quieting turbulence of all kinds. She helps us remember that taking a moment to step outside our passions and calm down can enhance our creativity.*

MANDALA 24

Matangi Yantra (ninth of the Ten Mahavidyas). Matangi brings justice to those who deserve it, and grants wealth, psychic powers, and literary ability. With her "intoxicated limbs," she is a powerful creative force. Matangi reminds us that even when we find ourselves at a disadvantage in a situation, we have options.

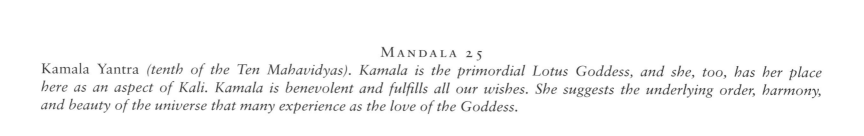

MANDALA 25

Kamala Yantra *(tenth of the Ten Mahavidyas). Kamala is the primordial Lotus Goddess, and she, too, has her place here as an aspect of Kali. Kamala is benevolent and fulfills all our wishes. She suggests the underlying order, harmony, and beauty of the universe that many experience as the love of the Goddess.*

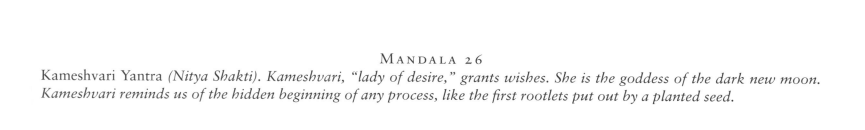

MANDALA 26

Kameshvari Yantra *(Nitya Shakti). Kameshvari, "lady of desire," grants wishes. She is the goddess of the dark new moon. Kameshvari reminds us of the hidden beginning of any process, like the first rootlets put out by a planted seed.*

Bhagamalini *(Nitya Shakti). Bhagamalini, whose name refers to the flowering* yoni *(vulva), arouses and incites. She is a goddess of the waxing moon. Bhagamalini suggests the gathering of one's resources for creating something new.*

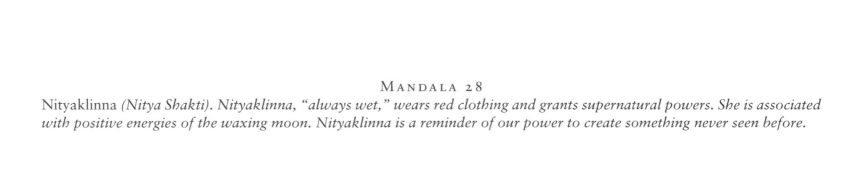

MANDALA 28

Nityaklinna *(Nitya Shakti). Nityaklinna, "always wet," wears red clothing and grants supernatural powers. She is associated with positive energies of the waxing moon. Nityaklinna is a reminder of our power to create something never seen before.*

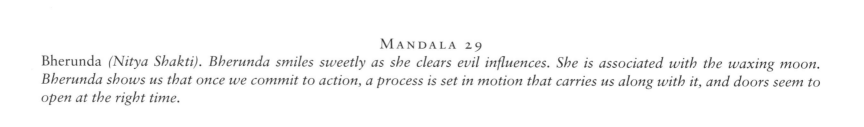

MANDALA 29

Bherunda *(Nitya Shakti). Bherunda smiles sweetly as she clears evil influences. She is associated with the waxing moon. Bherunda shows us that once we commit to action, a process is set in motion that carries us along with it, and doors seem to open at the right time.*

Mandala 30

Vahnivasini (Nitya Shakti). Vahnivasini, "dweller in fire," dresses in yellow silk garments. She grants mastery over the forces of nature as a goddess of the waxing moon. Vahnivasini conveys the intensity and excitement of bringing something new into being.

Mahavajeshvari *(Nitya Shakti). Mahavajeshvari banishes cruelty. She wears a crown of rubies as she presides over her phase of the waxing moon. As we step into our creative power, self-doubts may be triggered, but these need not be a hindrance.*

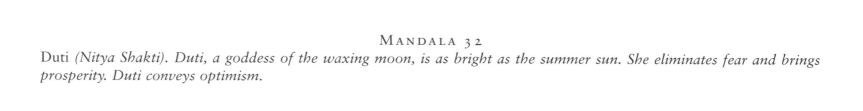

MANDALA 32

Duti *(Nitya Shakti). Duti, a goddess of the waxing moon, is as bright as the summer sun. She eliminates fear and brings prosperity. Duti conveys optimism.*

MANDALA 33

Tvarita (Nitya Shakti). Tvarita, whose name means "swift," is dark, youthful, and clad in new leaves. She wears a crest of peacock feathers. Tvarita quickly expands one's abilities to learn and bestows beauty and fame. She reminds us that the process of creating something also transforms us.

MANDALA 34

Kulasundari *(Nitya Shakti). Kulasundari, "beautiful heart," gives the reward of esoteric knowledge. She is associated with the waxing moon. Kulasundari suggests that wisdom comes from taking a loving approach to life.*

MANDALA 35

Nitya-Nitya (Nitya Shakti). Nitya-Nitya is a beneficent goddess of the waxing moon. She is dressed in red, like the dawn sun. Nitya-Nitya reminds us that our role as creators calls on us to witness, to acknowledge, and to accept our creations.

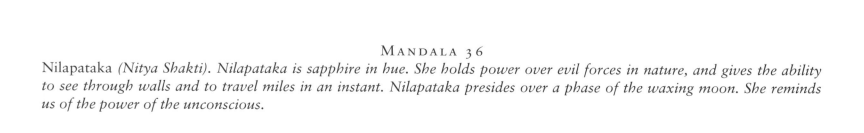

MANDALA 36

Nilapataka *(Nitya Shakti). Nilapataka is sapphire in hue. She holds power over evil forces in nature, and gives the ability to see through walls and to travel miles in an instant. Nilapataka presides over a phase of the waxing moon. She reminds us of the power of the unconscious.*

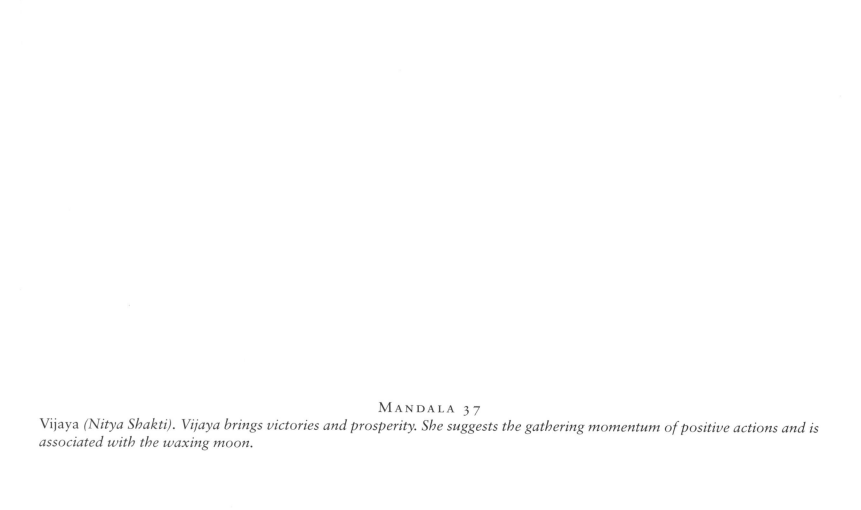

MANDALA 37

Vijaya *(Nitya Shakti)*. *Vijaya brings victories and prosperity. She suggests the gathering momentum of positive actions and is associated with the waxing moon.*

MANDALA 38

Sarvamangala *(Nitya Shakti). Sarvamangala, "all-auspicious," is wholly beneficent. She presides over the* kalas *(parts or digits) of the moon, the sun, and of fire. Sarvamangala reminds us of all that is lovely, orderly, and harmonious in the natural rhythms of the universe.*

MANDALA 39

Jvalamalini *(Nitya Shakti). Jvalamalini, "garlanded with flame," gives spiritually beneficial knowledge of previous births. She is associated with a phase of the waxing moon. Jvalamalini brings to mind the healing effect of making peace with one's past experiences.*

MANDALA 40

Chitra *(Nitya Shakti). Chitra, "variegated," is dressed in a rainbow of colors. She provides that which is desired, and banishes fear as she presides over a phase of the waxing moon. Chitra calls attention to the peaceful feeling of completing a creative process.*

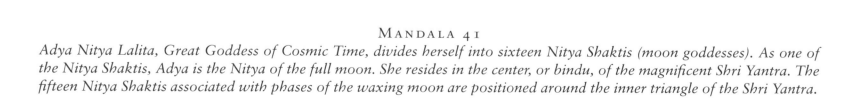

MANDALA 41

Adya Nitya Lalita, Great Goddess of Cosmic Time, divides herself into sixteen Nitya Shaktis (moon goddesses). As one of the Nitya Shaktis, Adya is the Nitya of the full moon. She resides in the center, or bindu, of the magnificent Shri Yantra. The fifteen Nitya Shaktis associated with phases of the waxing moon are positioned around the inner triangle of the Shri Yantra.

MANDALA 42

The Tibetan Buddhist goddess Lhamo, reminiscent of Kali, holds a skull cup and rides her mule rough-shod, crushing "the host of passion." She is a wrathful deity whose purpose is helpful. Her function is to tame and pacify all negative forces that, manifesting as activities and tendencies of the mind, bind us to the cycle of life and death.

MANDALA 43
The goddess Tara is a kind protectress who brings you just what you need for healing, enlightenment, and protection.

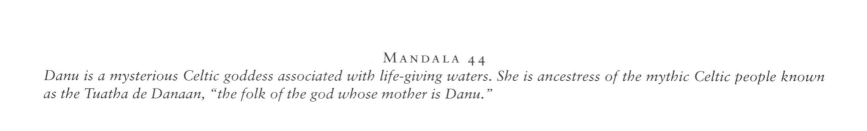

MANDALA 44

Danu is a mysterious Celtic goddess associated with life-giving waters. She is ancestress of the mythic Celtic people known as the Tuatha de Danaan, "the folk of the god whose mother is Danu."

MANDALA 45

Mandala of the Inner Diamond. *The interpenetrating triangles suggest the merging of opposing forces into a unified design around a gemlike center.*

MANDALA 46

Mandala of the Graceful Flower. *Circle drawing spins this graceful flower into the center of a design reminiscent of Islamic compositions.*

For Those Who Wish to Draw a Mandala

Circles have the special quality of gathering in, containing, protecting. A circle organizes whatever is inside it and establishes a sense of order. Circles are drawn from a center point, and even empty circles suggest their unseen center. Marking the center point in a mandala brings the whole design into harmonious relationship. With the assistance of simple drawing instruments that were technological marvels of the ancient world, it is possible to make the precise lines, measurements, and orderly patterns once used to call forth and express the essence of the Goddess. The mandalas for which drawing instructions are given are based on traditional designs that dazzle the senses and explode with visual possibilities, yet hold together within the ineffable gestalt of the circle.

You will need these materials: drawing pencil, eraser, ruler, and compass with screw adjustments. To help you get started, the last four circles of the coloring section (mandalas 47–50) are blank. You will find it helpful to number in light pencil the points on these blank mandalas, as shown around the circumference of the circle in the basic grid presented here. Begin by making a similar basic grid for your mandala, using a straightedge to draw light pencil lines between opposite points on the circle (for example, between 1 and 9, 2 and 10, and so on). The center of the circle will be at the point where all lines intersect. Mark the center with a small dot.

Specific instructions for mandalas 47 and 48 appear opposite the blank circles. Mandalas 49 and 50 are for you to improvise on your own. And finally, we've included two extra circles as a basis for any kind of mandala you'd like to create, whether drawn geometrically or colored wildly outside the lines.

Remember: There is no right or wrong way to create mandalas. Let them serve as a way to express your sacred feminine.

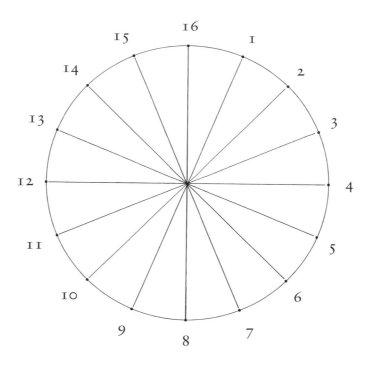

BASIC GRID FOR DRAWING MANDALAS

MANDALA 47

Try your hand at drawing the Mandala of the Inner Diamond *(mandala 45). Begin by drawing lines between points 3 and 13, 13 and 8, and 8 and 3. Next, draw lines between points 16 and 5, 5 and 11, and 11 and 16. From the intersection of lines 16–8 and 5–11, draw a line to point 2, and another to point 14. Now draw lines between points 2 and 14. From the intersection of lines 16–8 and 3–13, draw a line to point 6, and another to point 10. Then draw a line between 6 and 10. Mark the center point of your mandala. Place your compass point on the center and scribe a circle about one-half inch outside the circle given. Erase the penciled grid lines you do not want. Your mandala is ready for coloring.*

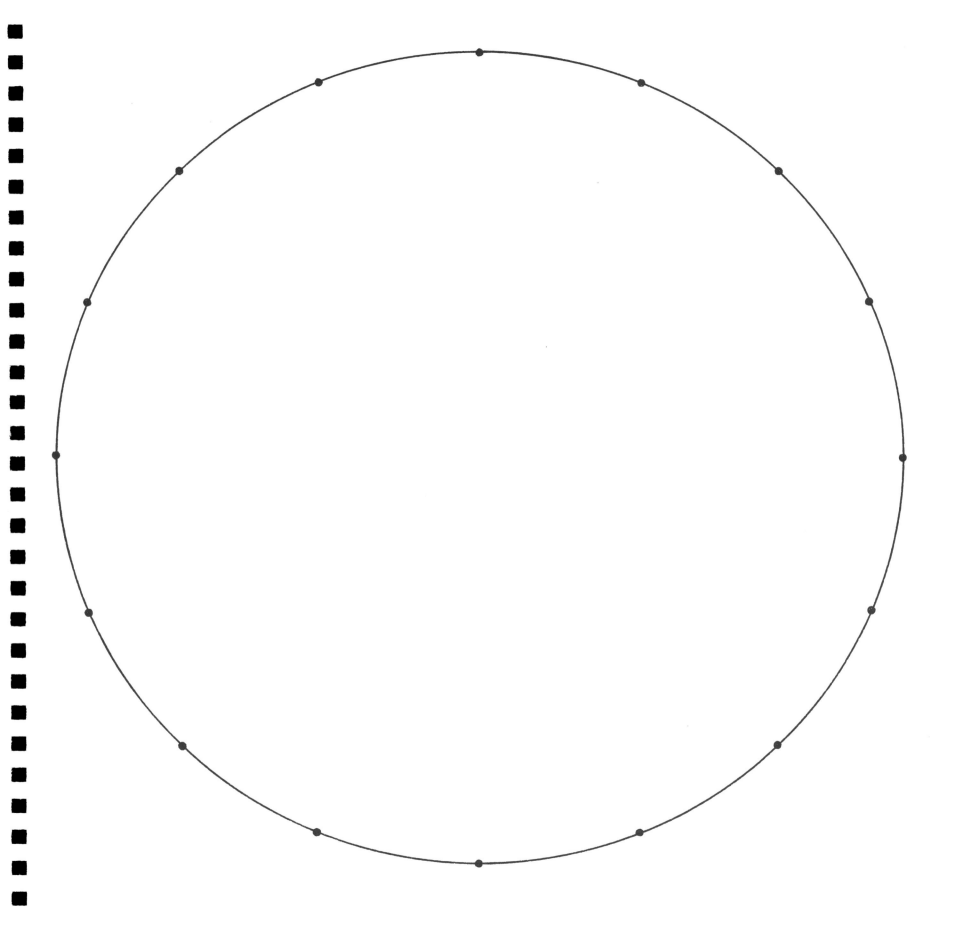

MANDALA 48

Try your hand at drawing the Mandala of the Graceful Flower *(mandala 46). Measure the distance between the center and point 4. Set your compass for half that distance. Place the point of your compass at the center point and scribe a circle. This is the inner circle. Place the point of your compass at the intersection of line 16–8 and the inner circle you just drew. Scribe a circle. Continue in the same way, placing the point of your compass at the intersection of line 2–10 and the inner circle. Draw a circle. Continue drawing circles from intersections of inner circle with lines 4–12, 6–14, 8–16, 10–2, 12–4, and 14–6. Erase grid lines. Your mandala is ready for coloring.*

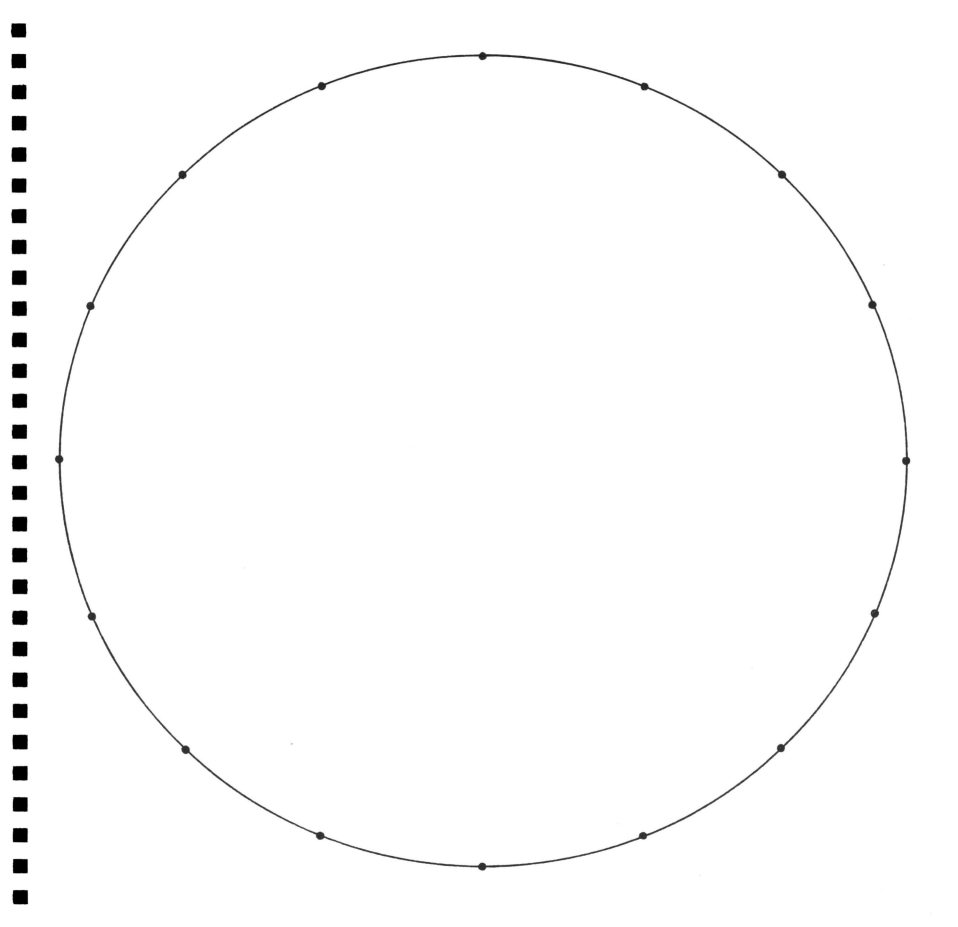

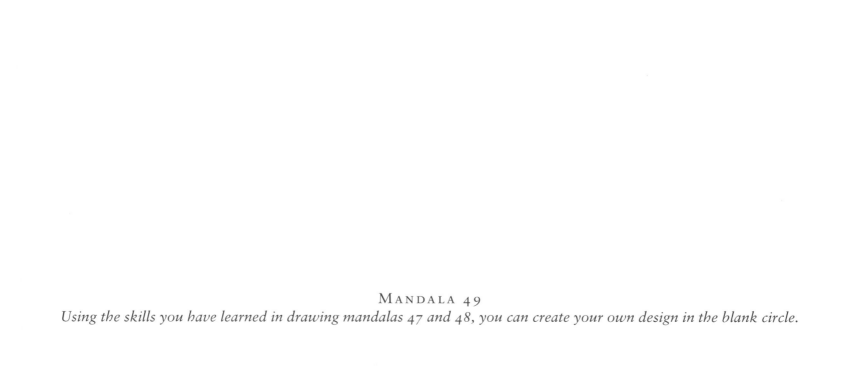

MANDALA 49
Using the skills you have learned in drawing mandalas 47 and 48, you can create your own design in the blank circle.

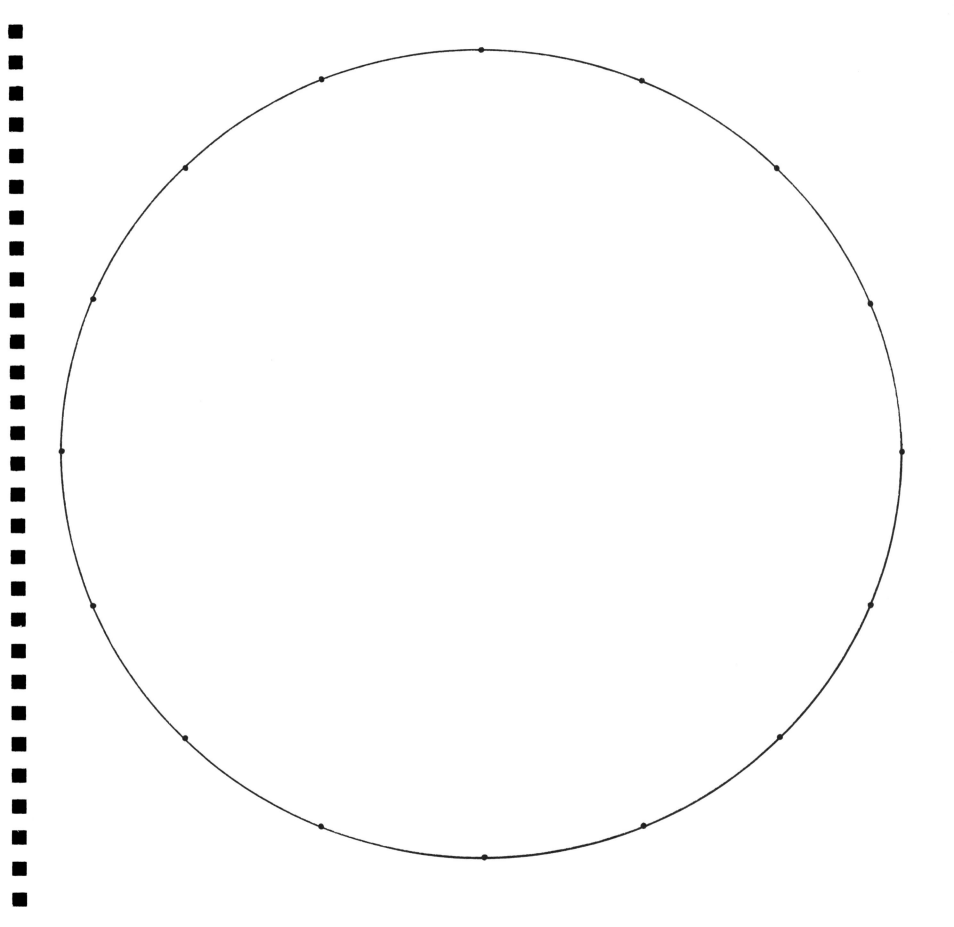

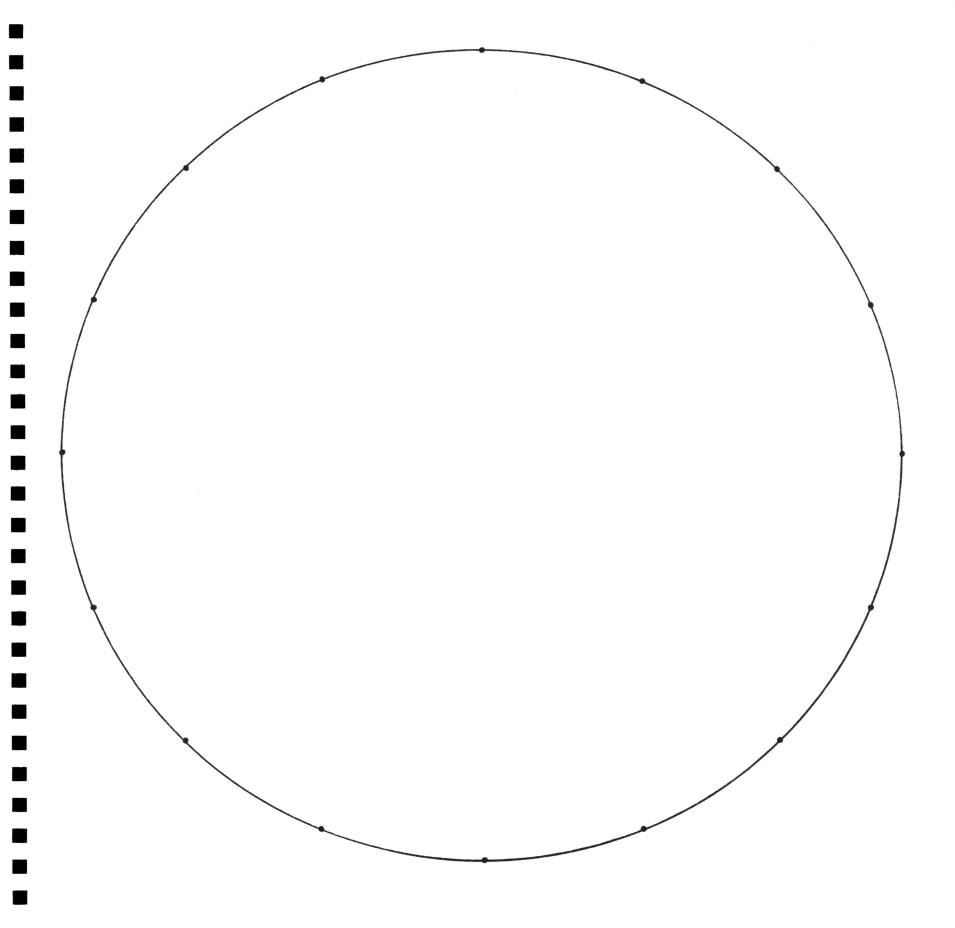

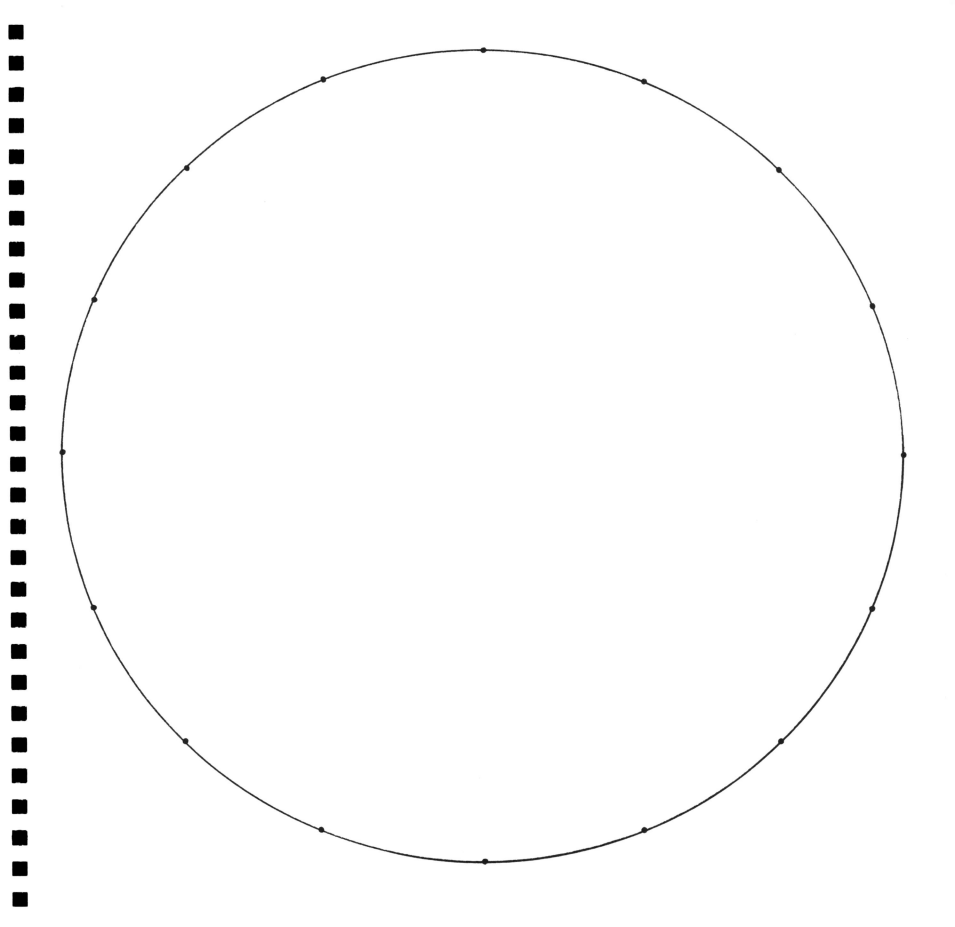

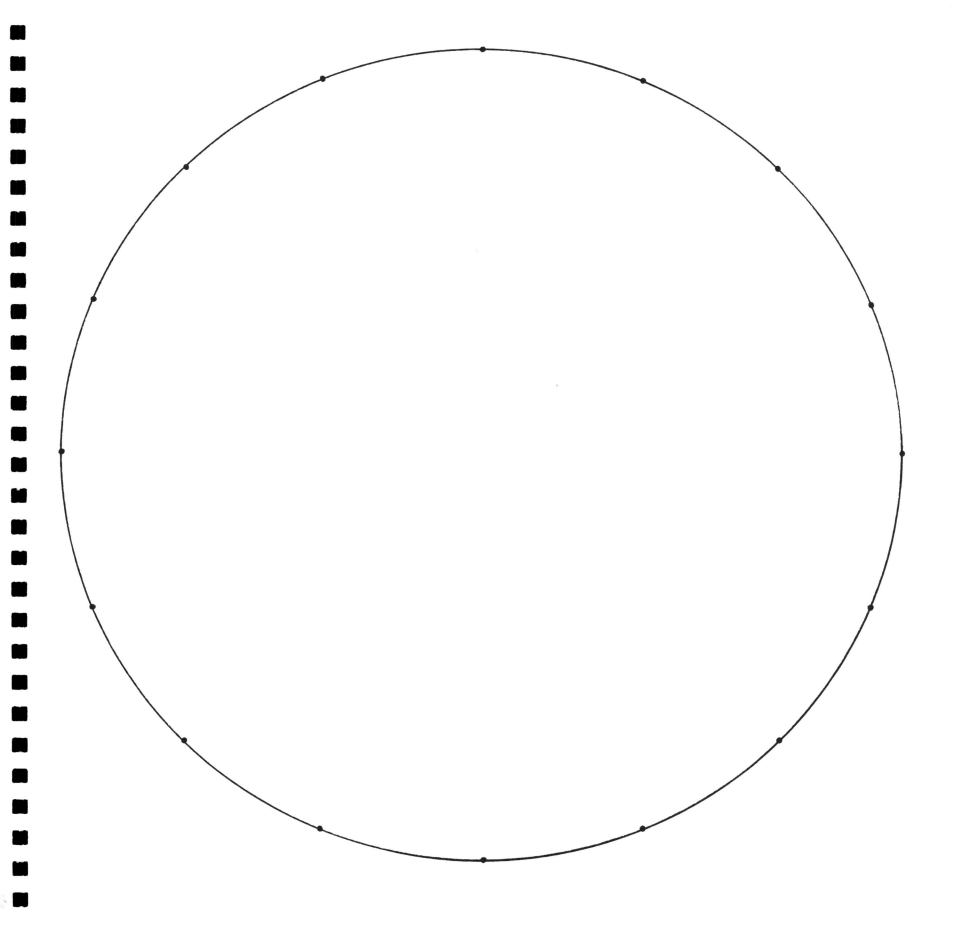